Matt,

I pray this book will
be a blessing to you as
you continue to seek to
be the best Dad, Husband
and Christian you can be.

Love,
Dad

MEN'S RELATIONAL TOOLBOX

GARY, GREG, AND MICHAEL SMALLEY

Tyndale House Publishers, Inc.
WHEATON, ILLINOIS

Visit Tyndale's exciting Web site at www.tyndale.com

Men's Relational Toolbox

Copyright © 2003 by Smalley Publishing Group, LLC. All rights reserved.

Cover and interior photographs of the toolbox © by Photodisc/Getty Images. All rights reserved.

Cover background photograph © 2003 by Dan Stultz. All rights reserved.

Gary Smalley photograph © 1999 by Jim Lersh. All rights reserved.

Greg Smalley and Michael Smalley photographs © 2001 by Jim Lersh. All rights reserved.

Published in association with the literary agency of Alive Communications, Inc., 7680 Goddard Street, Suite 200, Colorado Springs, CO 80920.

Designed by Ron Kaufmann

Edited by Lynn Vanderzalm and Tracy Sumner

The names and some of the details in the illustrations used in this book have been changed to protect the privacy of the people who shared their stories with us.

Unless otherwise indicated, all Scripture quotations are taken from the *Holy Bible,* New International Version®. NIV®. Copyright © 1973, 1978, 1984 by International Bible Society. Used by permission of Zondervan Publishing House. All rights reserved.

Scripture quotations marked NLT are taken from the *Holy Bible,* New Living Translation, copyright © 1996. Used by permission of Tyndale House Publishers, Inc., Wheaton, Illinois 60189. All rights reserved.

Scripture quotations marked "NKJV" are taken from the New King James Version. Copyright © 1979, 1980, 1982, 1991 by Thomas Nelson, Inc. Used by permission. All rights reserved.

Library of Congress Cataloging-in-Publication Data

Smalley, Gary.
  Men's relational toolbox / Gary, Greg, and Michael Smalley.
    p. cm.
Includes bibliographical references.
ISBN 0-8423-7445-0 (hc)—ISBN 0-8423-8320-4 (sc)
1. Christian men—Religious life. 2. Man-woman relationships—Religious aspects—Christianity.
3. Interpersonal relations—Religious aspects—Christianity. I. Smalley, Greg. II. Smalley, Michael. III. Title.

BV4528.2 .S52 2003
158.2'081—dc21   2002152234

Printed in the United States of America

08 07 06 05 04 03
8   7   6   5   4   3   2   1

We dedicate this book to several men
who have touched our lives:

to Jack Herschend, a great example of a loving husband;

to Dr. Gary Oliver, a mentor and friend;

to Brandon White and Jason Brawner, loyal friends.

Contents

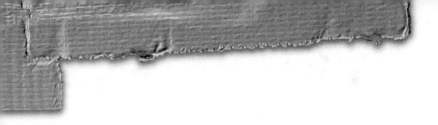

Acknowledgments

We've enjoyed working on this book—the first of many we hope to do together. As always, we could not have written this book without the help of some important people:

We thank Karen Kingsbury—an exceptionally gifted fiction writer—for her collaboration with us on this project. Karen, you captured our voices and made the book sing.

We thank our agent, Greg Johnson, for helping us brainstorm about the book and for encouraging us during the process.

Once again we thank our friends at Tyndale House Publishers for their partnership with us. Ken Petersen, thanks for inspiring and nurturing us during the writing of this book. Thanks to Lynn Vanderzalm, who is the best and most loving editor we know. Thanks also to Tracy Sumner for his editorial help.

Most important, we thank our wives, who daily stand with us and encourage us in the ministry God has entrusted to us. Norma, Erin, and Amy, thanks for your patience, your boundless love, and your devotion to us. God has used you to shape our lives.

The Smalley guys

Introduction

Something We're Good At

If you've been paying attention to my messages on love and relationships these past thirty years, you know one thing for sure—I don't have it all together. In fact, I've made my living reporting not just my failures as a husband and father but also the ways God helped me use those failures to restore the relationships between my family and me.

So why do you want to hear from a rusty old nail like me?

Because it warms your heart to know that if I can blunder my way through love and survive, so can you. The process has been riddled with laughter and tears, but the reward has always been gaining understanding about relationships.

Like any dad, I've tried to pass on what I know to my adult sons—Greg and Michael. And like any dad, I've done more than pass on the good stuff. That's right: God has a sense of humor, and Greg and Michael are just like me—two more rusty nails in the Smalley toolbox. Here's the proof:

✗ Not long after Greg and Erin got married, they were one argument away from splitting up.
✗ Michael wasn't speaking to his new bride eighteen hours after the wedding ceremony. He and Amy spent their first six months together camped on the rocks of discontent.

But there's good news too. Even though we are a trio of rusty nails, we're willing to do whatever we can to get our relationships right. And that's what this book is about—helping you develop your own relational toolbox that will help you make all your relationships exciting and successful.

My sons and I may be rusty nails, but when we realize we need to add the right relational tools, we're willing to do whatever we can to get the ones we need.

So you see, the beat goes on. And the message I bring you about building your relationships is now made three times stronger by the efforts of my sons. Yes, we still bumble our way through conversations with our wives every now and then. But we've learned something about relational tools, and it's this: With the right tools, we can build stronger, better relationships than we had before.

That's what we want to share with you in the pages of this book.

The information here will not answer all of your questions or solve all of your problems, but it will equip you with the tools to truly love and understand the people who are most important to you.

Now let us tell you a little bit about how this book came to be.

It happened one weekend when we three Smalley guys were together. Instead of swapping boasts about who had the better jump shot or the sweeter swing on the golf course, we were brainstorming.

We had been asked to write a relationship book for guys. Our conversation went something like this:

"I don't know if I can do it," Greg said as he stretched out his legs. "I'm tired of men-bashing books."

"Yeah, I'm tired of being portrayed as the 1940s inept relational guy. Things have changed. Men aren't bumbling idiots when it comes to relationships. We're just different from women," Michael said. "Can't we write a book about guys and relationships without coming off like a bunch of well-meaning, bumbling idiots?"

"Can't we write a book about our good points?" Greg suggested. "The reasons we excel as providers, protectors—that kind of thing?"

We started to catch Greg's passion. "You mean, take a look at our strengths, at why we're good at certain things?" I asked.

Greg was on his feet. "Exactly!" he said. "Why are we good at providing, for instance?"

"Because we have the tools for it," I said. "God-given tools."

"You're right," Greg said and pointed at me. "The take-charge tool, the fact-finding tool, the competitive-drive tool, the problem-solving tool."

"There it is!" Michael said. "Of course, our tools don't work in a relationship. We need other tools for that."

"When you build or repair something," I said, "what's the first thing you ask yourself?"

Greg grinned. "Do I have the right tools?"

"Yes!" I answered. "See, we're good at using the right tools for a lot of really important jobs. But maybe not the tools we need for relationships."

"And if you don't have the right tools . . . ?" Greg began.

"You get them!" Michael interrupted.

"Right!" I said. "We already have a fantastic, God-given internal toolbox. For most of us it's just a matter of adding a few more tools. The patient-listening tool, the tender-touch tool, the open-sharing tool. Things that'll help us relate better."

"But where does a guy find these new tools?" Michael asked.

And then it happened.

In a moment that seemed frozen in time, the three of us looked at each other and said in the same breath, "The Bible!"

"With our relationship book as a kind of instruction manual," I added.

And in that instant, the idea for this book was born.

The three of us agree on all the material in this book. It's what we're using today at the Smalley Relationship Center. In fact, it's the core of who we are as a team of relationship counselors. For that reason, we'll talk in this book in terms of *we* and *us*. We'll offer things we've seen, things we've picked up, research we've conducted—that kind of thing. All three of us have been counseling men about their relationships for years.

But until that conversation, it didn't hit us what we've really been doing.

We've been giving men tools. Relational tools.

You may already have some of these tools. Others you may need to add to your relational toolbox. If that's the case, consider the following pages your one-stop-shopping place when it comes to matters of relating. This book features tools you may never have considered, and it tells you how—through God's grace—you can own them free and clear.

GUY FACT

A man's self-esteem is career related.

If your relational toolbox has rusty hinges, you may need a full-scale shopping spree. Even the best of us struggle in one or two areas of relating to those we love. But we've found that those areas are often weaknesses that—with the proper tools—can become strengths.

Ever tried to use a pair of pliers to drive a nail into a stud? Once when Greg's hammer was missing, that's exactly what he did. The results? A crooked nail, a bruised thumb, and a heavy dose of frustration.

Why? Because he didn't use the right tool.

The same is true with relating. Without the right relational tools, we're going to struggle when it comes to building relationships. It's that simple.

So grab your toolbox and follow us. You're about to embark on a tool-gathering trip that will help you build or repair any relationship. Along the way, we've tried to make the journey a bit more fun by including stories, warnings, and tool tips. For those of you who like facts (Greg loves this sort of thing), we've included "guy facts" in the margins—fun, zany facts about . . . well, just about anything.

But before we go shopping, let's take a look at the tools you're already familiar with, the tools most of you have and use well.

After all, the last thing we want is another men-bashing book.

Rummaging through the Toolbox

It all centers on the toolbox.

After thousands of hours researching relationships and thousands more counseling others about them, we've stumbled onto a truth we believe can help any man build or repair his relationships. The truth is this: We build and repair our relationships much the same way we build and repair anything else—by using the right tools.

That's right. Our ability to effectively build or repair our relationships depends on the quality and number of items in what we call our "relational toolbox."

If you want to build or repair a deck around your house, you need a box full of the right kind of tools. The same is true if you want to build or repair a relationship. However, the problem with many of us guys is that we lack the right relational tools for the job. That doesn't make us the dimmest lights in the harbor. It makes us different.

For every relational tool we guys might lack, we possess a different internal tool—usually a factual and practical tool that makes us independent and skilled at providing and protecting, the two things most of us are best at.

Throughout the first half of this book we'll be discussing the internal tools that make us good providers and protectors. Then we'll take a look at those much-needed relational tools and take you on the ultimate shopping trip—the one that will equip you with the tools that will make you a better relationship builder and repairer.

GUY FACT

A man's sense of self is defined through his ability to achieve results, through success and accomplishment.

But before we do that, let's take a look at the other toolbox—the one sitting on the shelf in your garage.

A GUY'S NEED FOR TOOLS

Robert is a teacher, a guy whose most dangerous work tool is a pencil. He spends his hours instructing students about the wily ways of the English language. But like most guys, Robert has a toolbox on the garage shelf at home.

One day Robert's wife took the car on a carefree trip to the supermarket with their three toddlers buckled in the backseat. Unfortunately, she forgot to close the garage door when she left. When she and Robert met up at home at the end of the day, Robert announced that something tragic had happened.

His toolbox had been stolen.

To hear Robert's wife talk about his reaction, you'd have thought the house had burned down.

Robert stood in the garage, pacing in small circles, a vacant look in his eyes. "My tools," he said over and over. "Someone took my tools."

Robert's wife felt bad about the incident, but she was still able—with very little effort—to put the matter out of her mind long enough to help the kids safely into the house, unload the groceries, and start dinner.

"She told me I could get *new* tools," Robert explained later. "Can you believe that? *New tools?* As if that would somehow replace the tools I'd lost."

Robert eventually became excited at the prospect of getting new tools, but he wasn't thinking about that in the minutes after he found out about the burglary. Standing there staring at the empty garage shelf where his toolbox once sat, he thought, *What if I need to fix something? What if something's loose or something squeaks or something falls off?*

We believe Robert speaks for most of us guys when he said to us, "Guys, I felt naked."

We men often feel this same sense of inadequacy when we try to build or fix important relationships. We often don't have the necessary relational tools, and that leaves us feeling as helpless as Robert felt without his toolbox.

We may not be builders or mechanics or carpenters, but we feel secure knowing our toolbox is out there in the garage. It's reassuring, giving a sense of completeness. And we believe you can have that same feeling once you get to the second half of this book and stock your internal toolbox with the right relational tools.

GUY FACT

Two out of five husbands daily tell their wives that they love them.

If you checked inside the toolbox belonging to the average guy, you'd probably find some basic tools, including the following:

Hammer—used to pound or deliver repeated blows, especially when driving nails into wood

Wrench—usually operated by hand, used for tightening bolts and nuts

Screwdriver—used for turning screws with slotted heads

Pliers—used for holding and gripping small articles or bending and cutting wire

Tape measure—used for measuring

Saw—used for cutting solid materials to prescribed lengths or shapes

Lots of guys we know never build things and rarely even repair them. But almost every guy has a toolbox with at least these tools. Most of us aren't sure when we actually acquired our toolboxes, but we have them all the same. It's almost as though we woke up one morning and there in the garage was a toolbox with the basic tools that go along with being a man.

Why is this?

Because there are some things most guys are good at, and one of them is using tools to build and repair things. Our guess is that whether you are an accountant or a truck driver, a doctor or a delivery guy, you have a toolbox stocked with tools that you know how to use to accomplish some basic tasks.

Here's a list of the things most guys can do with the basic tools in their toolboxes:

- ✗ Hang a picture
- ✗ Install basic shelving
- ✗ Tighten and loosen things (like door hinges)
- ✗ Install a screen door
- ✗ Replace a faucet
- ✗ Change furnace filters
- ✗ Install a new light fixture
- ✗ Fix a broken toy
- ✗ Repair a leak
- ✗ Measure the size of a room or window
- ✗ Trim or cut a piece of wood
- ✗ Grip or hold something steady as it is being repaired

Now granted, you might be the kind of man who has traded in his toolbox for a tool chest, the man who has enough tools to allow you to assemble a 747 in your garage. But even if you can't tell the difference between a ratchet and a crescent wrench, you can usually handle the tasks listed above.

Certainly some guys don't own toolboxes—though we'd venture to say that they are for the most part, very young or very old guys. And we're equally certain some women have toolboxes like the one described above. But for the purposes of this book, we'll generalize a bit and say this: Toolboxes are primarily a guy thing.

There's a reason for this: Men and women are different.

This is probably not earth-shattering information to most people. In fact, you are probably nodding in agreement as you read this, not dropping the book in astonishment.

Sadly, when most people talk about the differences between men and women, it's usually in negative terms. We see women as having an "inborn relationship manual," while we see men as stumbling about looking for ways to get along in their relationships.

Or, as Greg said, we men-bash.

We aren't going to do that in this book. Instead, we will take a look at what we're trying to build. This book is a manual for building relationships, mostly relationships with women—girlfriends, wives, mothers, daughters, coworkers, bosses, committee members. Of course, guys need relational tools to relate with other men, but generally guys are already equipped with the tools necessary to do that. The relational tools that work between guys will not always work when a man tries to relate to a woman. In fact, that kind of relationship usually requires a different set of tools altogether.

With that in mind, let's look at our internal makeup and at what types of tools we guys have in our internal toolbox.

That's right—our internal toolbox.

THE INTERNAL TOOLBOX

Men are born with an internal toolbox. Internal tools are as important to us men as our toolbox out in the garage.

They are so important that if we woke up one day and didn't have these tools, we'd be lost, just as lost as Robert was when he discovered his toolbox had been stolen.

Just like a man who once lost his tool pouch. The story played out this way.

A female friend of ours had an appointment at the local middle school. She was waiting at the office counter when a man dressed in a suit and tie rushed in. He was breathless, and sweat was dripping off his forehead. In his hand was something large and cumbersome—about the size of a grocery bag. At first our friend couldn't quite make out what it was.

"Here you go," he said as he held it up.

His tone was similar to the one a man uses when he's bagged a five-point buck. But our friend could see that this man wasn't carrying a deer. He held in his hands a large tool pouch overflowing with wrenches, drills, pliers, and other assorted tools. Our friend noted that none of the tools looked even close to new. "The contents were worn out and dirty, like leftover clutter from a garage sale," she said later.

We know what most of you guys are thinking. *Tools? Like leftover clutter from a garage sale? Hardly!*

The businessman held up the tool pouch for the women behind the counter to see. "I found this in front of your school. It was just *lying* there on the sidewalk," he said incredulously, shaking his head.

The women in the school office glanced from the man to the tool pouch and back again, their faces utterly blank. They were probably thinking what our friend was thinking—that whoever left the pouch had obviously done so on purpose. Maybe it had gotten too heavy to carry another few blocks down the road to the Goodwill truck.

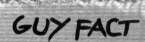

GUY FACT

In 1838 the city of Los Angeles passed an ordinance requiring that a man obtain a license before serenading a woman.

Finally, one of the women stepped forward. "Okay. What should we do with it?" she asked.

Now the blank stare belonged to the man. "These are *tools!*" he said.

His tone suggested that losing tools might be only slightly less tragic than losing a child, but definitely worse than, say, losing a wedding ring or a thousand dollars cash.

The woman at the counter was not seeing that.

"Well," the other woman said as she peered into the tool pouch, her nose slightly wrinkled, "okay."

Now the man huffed, "Look, I'm late for the biggest appointment of my life, lady. But I had to stop. Somewhere there's a guy *missing* these tools." He said the word *missing* with a level of emotion usually reserved for weddings and funerals. "I couldn't drive another foot without stopping," he said and motioned back to where his car was parked. "I ran all the way up here."

The woman used her toe to point to a spot on the floor. "Put them there, I guess," she said. "Maybe someone will claim them."

"*Maybe* someone will—" the man stopped himself. "Never mind. I'm late for work."

He turned and ran out of the school, hair disheveled, coat tails flapping in the wind. But he had a heroic look on his face, as if he'd done a deed that made him worthy of calling himself a man.

After he left, the woman behind the counter turned to her office coworker and said, "Is it just me, or was that man a little over-the-top about tools?"

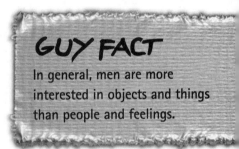

GUY FACT

In general, men are more interested in objects and things than people and feelings.

The fact is, most of us guys are a little over-the-top about the tools in our toolboxes. It's the same way when it comes to our internal tools.

The good news is we excel at something. In fact, in some settings we're downright amazing. That's because our internal toolbox contains certain tools that make us naturals in those settings.

Let's take a look at some of the internal tools you probably already have.

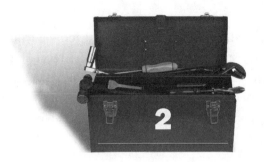

A Man's Internal Tools

Picture an imaginary toolbox located somewhere in your chest. Now imagine yourself opening the lid and peering inside. What's there? Let's take a look at the internal tools we already have and know how to use.

In addition to the internal tools we are naturally equipped with, most of us have something else there too: extra space. That's where your relational tools will go when we get to that section later.

But for now let's just rummage through the toolbox and see what's there. What most of us will find are tools that help us accomplish the tasks God designed us to accomplish. Here is a list of the six basic internal tools that are standard equipment for most guys:

✗ Fact-giving tool
✗ Fact-finding tool
✗ Take-charge tool
✗ Task-oriented tool
✗ Problem-solving tool
✗ Competitive-drive tool

You may notice that the first two internal tools on this list deal with communication, specifically with giving and receiving information. We use the other four tools to accomplish the tasks guys need to accomplish. But most of the time these six tools work together to do something in the typical man: give him a strong sense of individuality and independence.

INDEPENDENCE—MASTERY OF A GUY'S INTERNAL TOOLS

The man who masters the use of tools in the garage or on a building site might become a mechanic or a builder. But the man who becomes expert with these internal tools becomes something altogether different: independent.

It's important for us guys to remember that we have a great need for *independence;* we value being separate and different. However, women have a great need for *intimacy* and *connection;* they value being close and similar. Do you see the difference in these needs and values? Can you see how they can lead to misunderstanding and disappointment?

We men need to understand that the use of our internal tools creates a posture of independence. That independence can look like self-reliance, self-sufficiency, or autonomy. Men are conditioned at work to function independently. We are told, "You do your job, and I'll do mine." To be competent providers and protectors, we must be able to function independently. This is a God-given need.

But this conflicts with a woman's need for connection. And our internal tools, instead of drawing us toward relational connection, drive us toward independence. In the workplace men need to connect—to "talk" about things—only when something is wrong, when a problem arises, or when they're not doing their job well. The implication is that when women want to connect at home by talking about tasks, men tend to hear this message: "Something is wrong" or "You're not doing your job well."

One night Julie started to talk to her husband about removing a stump from their lawn. Her goal was simply to talk in order to connect. But the moment she brought up the subject, her husband, Denny, became defensive and hurt. He assumed she was talking about it because she thought he was incompetent. He was conditioned to work independently ("You do your job, and I'll do mine"), so when she wanted to "discuss" things, he misunderstood her intentions and reacted.

Greg recounts similar situations with his wife, Erin. When he's at work, functioning in a you-do-your-job-and-I'll-do-mine mode, and Erin calls to discuss something about their children, he reacts. Instead of seeing the call as a chance to connect, he thinks, *I need you to do your job. When you call me about the kids, I feel as if I need to do my job and yours too!* Men often do not understand that women are successful at home because they connect by verbally processing things. When Erin called to talk about the kids, she was not asking Greg to do her job. She was merely trying to connect—to process verbally—so that she could do her job better.

Historically, researchers believed that both men and women respond to life's stresses the same way. Hormones are released that make the body so energized, it will either fight or flee. This behavior goes back to the days when humans had to hunt down their dinners and protect themselves from predators.

GUY FACT

Men rarely talk about their problems unless they are seeking "expert" advice. Asking for help when they can do something themselves is a sign of weakness.

But researchers at UCLA are beginning to believe that women have learned to react differently to stress. A five-year study found that women release a hormone called *oxytocin*, which supports a woman's tendency to unite with other women. Specifically, when women get stressed out, they get together with other women. In other words, they seek out relationships. Once the women are together, the oxytocin is released in their bodies in even higher doses, causing more peace and calm in their lives. Men don't have the advantage of experiencing the same level of calmness because their testosterone is counteracting any level of oxytocin. So when men get stressed out, they seek solitude or isolation.[1]

Women turn to each other to seek comfort and have someone else who can relate to their distinctive female attributes. In her book *Positive Solitude,* Rae André states that "Women develop more interpersonal skills than do men. From childhood on, men are oriented to seeing their world in terms of achievement, while women see their world in terms of relationships. Women are more in touch with the emotions on which relationships are based and because they expect one day to be alone, without an intimate partner, women usually develop better friendship-forming skills."[2]

What does it look like when a man acts out of independence? When a husband makes important family decisions by himself, acting as if he doesn't need help with anything, he communicates that his wife is not part of the team. As a result, she may see him as self-centered or self-focused, and misunderstandings follow.

We'll let Greg tell a story about when his independence got him into trouble.

Erin and I had been married for only a couple of months when someone introduced me to the wonderful world of home shopping through catalog companies. As I was looking through a catalog, I noticed that I could order bags of caramel corn. Since Erin and I love caramel corn, I figured that I would surprise her. Even though we were on a pretty tight budget and we had agreed to consult each other on major purchases, I still went ahead and ordered the caramel corn. The problem was that I didn't pay attention to what I was ordering and somehow got the order number mixed up. Several weeks later the UPS man showed up at our door. He informed Erin that we had a package but that he needed help bringing up the box.

When I came home that night, I bumped into the largest box I'd

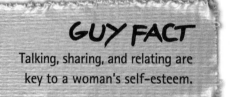

GUY FACT

Talking, sharing, and relating are key to a woman's self-esteem.

ever seen. My first thought was, *What on earth did Erin buy? She's in big trouble for not talking to me first!* Erin quickly informed me that *my* package had arrived. It was the caramel corn. But instead of the single tin I thought I had ordered, I faced a refrigerator-sized box of individual packages of caramel corn. We had hundreds of them—with no room to store them in our tiny studio apartment.

For the next several months we had caramel corn for nearly every meal. Friends started teasing us and saying things like, "Don't go over to the Smalleys. They'll try to send you home with bags of caramel corn." Needless to say, I haven't eaten caramel corn since that time.

Male independence expresses itself in a variety of ways, as the following three men illustrate:

✓ Harry heads up sales at a big corporation. He has more than mastered the fact-finding tool and the fact-giving tool. He routinely travels the globe making business connections and servicing the company's larger accounts. He has no trouble taking charge in a meeting or problem solving if a difficult issue arises. His coworkers look to him for wisdom and guidance. However, Harry and his wife are in counseling because they feel like strangers living in the same house. Harry hasn't connected emotionally with his wife or anyone else in years, and he wouldn't know how to do it if he were forced to. The problem? Harry is the picture of independence.

✓ Joe is a lawyer with the county's prosecuting office. By day he rattles off facts for various judges, and by night he researches the potential loopholes in his cases. He comes home and needs only a meal and a quick hug before he heads back to his office, where he continues to work. His problem-solving and task-oriented tools work in high gear every hour he's awake. Meanwhile, Joe's teenage daughter has become physically involved with her boyfriend and has recently announced that she is pregnant. The problem? Joe isn't emotionally available to his family, and his daughter fills that void with her boyfriend. Joe is devastated at this turn of events, but he doesn't see his role in creating the problem. In mastering his internal tools, Joe has become independence defined.

✓ Steve is a college basketball player. The competition is fierce, and he has disciplined himself to spend three hours a day working out alone in a gym near his house. He spends his evenings playing pickup ball with a few of the guys from the team. His afternoons are for homework—otherwise he won't keep his grades high enough to maintain his scholarship. Steve excels wildly at using the competitive-drive tool, and he's also an expert at utilizing the task-oriented tool, which helps him stay on target in the classroom. But Steve's personal relationships are suffering. His parents say they hardly know him, and even his teammates complain that he doesn't seem like part of the team. The reason? In his superb use of the competitive-drive tool, Steve has become a walking illustration of independence.

When these three men realized what had happened in their personal relationships, they wondered what they'd done wrong and what they could do to fix those relationships. "Maybe I should throw out my internal tools and start over," Steve said when we met with him.

TOOL TIP

Remember that your natural internal tools are useful and beneficial to you in many parts of your life.

But starting over is not the answer. And throwing away those internal tools isn't even an option. The actual solution is simpler than you think. It's just a matter of adding the right tools to your internal toolbox, then learning how to use those tools effectively.

Let us illustrate, again using the items in a literal toolbox.

If you needed to cut a piece of wood to a certain length but had only a hammer and wrench in your toolbox, would you throw out the hammer and wrench? Of course not! You'd simply head down to the hardware store and pick up a saw.

That's what you may need to do with your internal toolbox. It's not a matter of getting rid of anything but of adding to what you already have. That is exactly what we're going to do in the coming chapters. Once you understand a little more about the tools you already own, we'll take you shopping for a box full of relational tools. We'll talk about them at length later, but for now let's just throw them out on the table and see what we might need to add to our tool collection.

THE RELATIONAL TOOLS YOU MIGHT NEED TO ADD

We have compiled a list of six tools we believe can help any man become better at personal relationships. We also believe that any man can add these tools to his own internal toolbox, enabling him to relate better to those around him.

Here are the relational tools we're talking about:

✗ Open-sharing tool
✗ Patient-listening tool
✗ Win-win tool
✗ Selfless-honor tool
✗ Tender-touch tool
✗ Time-and-energy tool

There you have it. These are the tools that help us overcome our independence and make us more effective in our relationships. They have worked for us, and they can work for you!

Before we move on, let's make one thing clear: We'll be generalizing a lot in the next few chapters. We know that some men may not have all the usual "male" internal tools listed above, and we know that others may already have a significant number of relational tools. We also know that some women have internal tools that are similar to those of most men. For example, maybe a woman in your life is more factual or better at problem solving than you are. Either way, we're certain you'll see yourself somewhere in the following chapters. We also believe that along the way, you'll see several relational tools you can use. These are tools that can change your relationships forever.

Over the next few chapters, we will attempt to give you a better understanding of the internal tools most men already possess and why those tools work so well to do what men usually do best: provide and protect.

WHAT WE GUYS DO BEST: PROVIDE AND PROTECT

The internal tools most of us guys naturally possess and know how to use best are the ones that help us in doing the things God designed us to do: provide for our families and protect them.

Rhonda, a writer and speaker, is an emotional and deeply relational person; she's married to Sam, a basketball coach who generally sees most of life as a series of sports drills. While Rhonda wishes Sam had a more developed relational side, she will tell you that she's happy in her marriage.

GUY FACT

Most people eat about 60,000 pounds of food in their lifetime—the weight of about six elephants.

"I wish he were more emotional," Rhonda has said. "But I wouldn't want to be married to anyone else."

The reason? She'll be the first to tell you.

"He takes care of me and the kids. He's our provider and protector. That's how he loves us, and it means the world to me."

One night Rhonda realized just how important that provision and protection were to her. Sam had to attend an evening basketball meeting and wouldn't be home until late. Rhonda fixed dinner, fed the kids, bathed them, and put them to bed. Then she turned off the downstairs lights and headed upstairs to her office to do some writing before Sam got home.

Five minutes into her work, Rhonda heard a very loud scraping sound coming from outside the house. It was the kind of sound she might hear if, say, a burglar was trying to remove a screen from the living-room window and break into the house—or perhaps sharpen his machete against the patio door.

The sound came again.

Adrenaline shot through Rhonda's veins. She was suddenly terrified, barely able to breathe. Again and again the sound came. *Scraaape. Scrape, scrape, scrape. Scraaape. Scraaape. Scrape, scrape.* Rhonda's thoughts began running like a bad TV show.

The burglar thinks we're not home. . . . He couldn't get the window open, so now he's trying to pick the lock on the door. . . . Or maybe he's a kidnapper. . . . Maybe he knows we're home. Maybe he knows Sam's not here, and he's trying to break in with a hacksaw. . . . Maybe he'll take me and the kids to some undisclosed place and demand ransom money from Sam. . . . Maybe he's on his way up the stairs right now! If that happens I have to defend us! I must!

She glanced around her office, looking to find something—anything—to use as a weapon to ward off the threat. The most threatening weapon Rhonda could find was an unopened box of floppy disks. The sound continued at about half the speed of her racing heart, and she knew there was really only one way to save herself and her family.

She called 911.

Two squad cars pulled up to the front of the house just as Sam returned from his basketball meeting.

"What's going on?" Sam shouted as he jumped from his car.

"Someone's trying to break into the house," the officer reported, casting a suspicious look at Sam and asking to see his identification—just in case he turned out to be the prowler.

Sam checked out okay, and he joined the officers headed for the front door. There, a stricken-looking Rhonda greeted them, her face pale and her eyes wide. In her trembling hands was the box of floppy disks.

"He's in the backyard," was all she could manage.

Sam immediately took Rhonda in his arms and waited with her by the porch. The officers, with guns drawn, crept around the side of the house where the family's dog-run area was located.

That's when the officers heard the noise Rhonda had described. *Scraaape. Scrape, scrape.* Moving carefully, quietly, they stepped closer to the dog area. Then they saw and heard the source of the mysterious sound.

The noise was coming from the doghouse, which sat up against the side of Sam and Rhonda's home. As it turned out, Sam had given the family dog a steak bone before leaving for his meeting. In the dog's effort to chew off every last bit of meat from the bone, the eighty-pound Labrador retriever had spent most of the last hour adjusting his position in the doghouse to get the best angle on the bone. The dog's body brushed against the doghouse, which in turn bumped up against the outside wall of Sam and Rhonda's house. That was the source of the continuous scraping sound.

No burglar, no kidnapper, no hacksaw.

Just a determined dog.

Rhonda was more than a little red faced when the police officers returned to the front door and explained that her family was—strictly speaking—in very little danger. As long as they didn't try to take the bone away from their dog, that is.

Rhonda knew that if Sam had been home, the situation more than likely would have played out differently.

Sam and Rhonda would have been in their room, discussing the children or winding down at the end of the day. Suddenly the scraping sound would have caught their attention.

"What's that?" Rhonda would have asked, her face already showing concern.

"I don't know," Sam would have answered. "I'll go find out."

Using his fact-finding and problem-solving tools, Sam would

> **GUY FACT**
>
> In Pennsylvania, ministers are forbidden from performing marriages when either the bride or groom is drunk.

have slipped on a pair of shoes, headed downstairs, flung open the back door, and walked into the night, ready to face whatever was making the noise.

TOOL TIP

Most guys are naturally equipped to be providers and protectors, which is what God designed us to do within our families.

Sam would have seen that the dog was having a field day with his bone; then he would have returned to the bedroom and reported, "It was just the dog."

When Rhonda talks about Sam, it's with hero worship in her voice. It doesn't matter that she makes more money than he does. His internal tools—his ability to solve problems and find the facts, his knack at accomplishing a goal—have made him the family's provider and protector.

Just as God designed it.

WHERE OUR INTERNAL TOOLS WORK—AND DON'T WORK

We said earlier in this book that the last thing we want to do is bash men because of their need for relational tools. We're still holding to that! The internal tools most of us guys naturally possess equip us to do the things we were designed to do. Guys, keep in mind that you're very good at certain things:

✗ Researching and completing a report or project for your company
✗ Reaching or breaking your boss's sales quotient or expectations
✗ Figuring out why you aren't achieving a business goal
✗ Consistently showing up at work on time—day in, day out
✗ Fixing things or doing visible, obvious chores around the house
✗ Solving a problem with the children
✗ Locating the cause of any number of strange nighttime sounds

Here's the tricky part. As good as our internal tools are for helping us accomplish what are usually "guy things," we need a different set of tools if we're going to build satisfying relationships. And not only that, we need to learn to follow the instructions for using those tools.

Surely you've used the wrong tool for a job once or twice in your life, right? And if not, perhaps you've had the right tool but didn't follow the instructions for using that tool on a particular job.

We know we've done one or both those things before, and the outcome was never pretty. That was certainly the case for Ed, who had a great grip on how to use his internal tools but a considerably looser one on the tools he kept out in the garage. Here's what happened.

One Christmas Ed bought his children a swing set. His plan was to slip outside on Christmas Eve after the children were asleep and assemble the swing set. Since Ed lived in Arizona, he figured it would stay warm enough outside for him to finish the job without freezing.

> **GUY FACT**
>
> More Monopoly money is printed in a year than real money is printed throughout the world!

Now, Ed was an accountant who rarely assembled anything more complex than a LEGO fort. Nevertheless, he fetched his toolbox from the shelf in the garage and set himself to the task.

"How hard could it be?" he asked his wife.

His wife rolled her eyes and reminded him of the rocking horse he'd assembled the previous Christmas—the one with the head on backward.

This, of course, brings us to the point about following directions. Even if we guys are up-to-speed on how to use the tools in our toolboxes, we don't always feel a great need to follow directions. Most jobs appear far too simple to spend upwards of fifteen minutes reading directions—or worse, trying to understand those simple diagrams. You know the ones—arrows this way and that, multiple steps, illustrations that make assembling a cardboard box akin to nuclear science.

In other words, sometimes it's easier just to look at the picture and wing it.

This is particularly true when it comes to assembling a child's toy. *It's just a toy,* we say to ourselves, and we grab hold of our task-oriented and problem-solving tools.

"Just do it!" is our motto at times like these. Especially when Christmas morning is mere hours away.

This was Ed's mind-set as he hauled the swing set box—a cardboard package bigger than his Honda—into the backyard just after nine o'clock on Christmas Eve. His wife followed him, ready to assist. Ed had given her the job of holding the flashlight while he assembled the swing set.

"What if it's more difficult than it looks?" she muttered.

But Ed was undaunted. He had hold of the task-oriented tool as well as the problem-solving tool, and he was ready to go. "Imagine their faces when they wake up Christmas morning and find a swing set where today there was just a patch of grass," Ed said. He could imagine the kids' excited expressions. He could hear their joyous cries of delight. Come morning he'd be a hero for sure.

GUY FACT

An old law on the books in Riverside, California, makes it illegal to kiss unless both the man and woman wipe their lips with rose water.

His wife positioned the light and asked, "What if it takes longer than you think?"

"We'll be done before midnight," he assured her. He opened the cardboard box and heaved out a two-foot-high bag full of nuts, bolts, chains, whosits, and whatsits. Then he took another careful look at the picture on the side of the box. "No problem!"

He had a mission, and nothing was going to get in his way.

His wife picked up the directions. "It says you need a ratchet set to assemble this, Ed," she pointed out. "Have you read the directions?"

"I don't need a ratchet set," Ed chuckled and began pulling out the steel swing set legs. "My tools will work just fine."

Using only his basic toolbox, four hours later Ed had the main beams and legs of the swing set completely assembled. But there was one small problem: The factory-built rings the swings were supposed to hang from were jutting out of the *top* of the main beam instead of hanging from the bottom.

Ed had installed the legs upside down.

This meant Ed's children would have two options. Either use the swing set only when gravity was not in effect or dig a swing-set-sized hole in the yard and allow the beam to balance across the top of it, the legs forming gigantic Vs at either end.

"Hmm," Ed said.

You guys know things have gotten bad when we say, "Hmm."

At this point Ed was in big trouble. And all because he didn't see the importance of reading the directions or using the correct tools.

With the swing set looking like an oversized piece of metallic artwork no more capable of supporting swings than, say, a clothesline, Ed's wife rolled her eyes again. She did not say a word. She just set down the flashlight, aimed it in Ed's direction, headed into the house, and went to sleep.

Because Ed's problem-solving tool was still in fine working order, he was able to summon the fortitude and patience to disassemble the swing set and, following the directions, put it together again—this time correctly.

As correctly as he could without the use of a ratchet set, that is.

At six in the morning—after finding out that December nights are indeed freezing cold, even in Arizona—Ed stumbled into his bedroom and nudged his wife.

"I did it," he said with pride in his voice, a tone that said, "I came, I saw, I conquered."

His wife rolled over and said, "Are the legs tight?"

Ed held his breath. This was not the type of information he wanted to reveal at that moment, after spending the entire night putting together a swing set. He cleared his throat. "Not exactly," he confessed.

"The kids can't play on it until you make it tight, Ed. It's not safe."

And that was that.

Ed's wife had a point: It's absolutely crucial that we use the proper tools if we plan on building something of quality. Like Ed, many of us guys have the energy, the patience, and the desire to pull off a certain project. But we simply lack the proper tools to finish what we set out to do, or we haven't taken the time to follow the instructions on how to use them.

GUY FACT

An American man once had the hiccups for sixty-nine years!

When it comes to building relationships, we can find the tools and the directions in God's Word. These things are absolutely essential to building quality personal relationships. They spell out clearly the relational tools we need in order to understand each other.

We'll talk about that more later on in this book, but for now let's continue examining the internal tools most men have and use.

THIS JUST ISN'T VERY HELPFUL!

As we pointed out before, there are many, many situations where the internal tools most men are equipped with are helpful, even necessary. But when it comes to personal relationships, those same internal tools can fall short.

Here are some of the settings in which the typical man's internal tools are not helpful:

✗ Sharing your own deep personal feelings and needs
✗ Developing an interest in another person's feelings and needs
✗ Understanding motivations of the heart
✗ Expressing the ways you value a person you love
✗ Developing close relationships with people you love

Doing the things listed above doesn't always come naturally for many of us guys. Does that make us bumblers? Not at all! It just means we need to equip ourselves to relate that way. We need to stock our internal toolbox with better relational tools, then learn how to use them.

Allow us to illustrate this point. If we told you we couldn't build a woodshed, you wouldn't condemn us as inept. Rather, you would tell us to obtain the correct directions and blueprints to build the shed, get the proper tools, and have at it. Even then, we may not become expert woodshed builders in a single weekend. But over time we'd grow more familiar with the directions and more adept with our new tools. Before long we could build as sound a woodshed as the next guy.

That's how it is with relationships too.

Once we have the right relational tools and directions, we can excel where before we failed. We will be equipped to build or repair any and all of our personal relationships. By the way, we have good news about Ed. The day after Christmas, he bought a ratchet set and tightened down the nuts, bolts, and screws on the children's swing set to a point where the swing set could not possibly be *unassembled*—not even in an emergency. Ed also offered his swing-set-assembling services to other fathers on the block. Pretty soon he had established a reputation for having the right tools and the ability to put together a swing set in two hours flat.

> **GUY FACT**
>
> Chewing gum while peeling onions will keep you from crying.

Ed was a picture of what can happen when a man takes the time to equip himself with the right tools and the proper instructions for a job. As you read on, you will see that the same can happen for you in your relationships.

But before we get into that, let's take a look at some of the research we've done on our internal tools and where they come from. We think the results will surprise you.

Looking Back: Where Did These Tools Come From?

In the first two chapters, we pointed out that we men have internal toolboxes that often lack certain tools necessary for relating on an emotional level to the ones we care about. But the questions remain, where did these internal toolboxes come from, and how did they develop?

We believe that you have to go clear back to Old Testament times in order to fully understand a man's need for the tools that still fill our internal toolboxes today. When we think about it, we shouldn't be surprised at the nature of the relational tools found in a man's internal toolbox. In fact, we'd go so far as to say that these tools have been part of a man's internal makeup for as far back as time itself.

If you doubt this, then take a stroll back through the Old Testament and look at some of the guys at work in biblical times. You'll see men providing and protecting, building and fighting. But you'll also see each of the typical guy's internal tools at work in dozens of situations.

Here are just a few biblical examples of men's internal tools at work:

✗ Before the Fall, Adam tended and kept the Garden (see Genesis 2:15).

✗ Before the Fall, Adam named the animals (see Genesis 2:19).

✗ After the Fall, Adam was instructed to till the ground (see Genesis 3:23).

✗ Cain worked the ground (see Genesis 4:2).

✗ Abel tended sheep (see Genesis 4:2).

✗ Noah built the ark (see Genesis 6–7).

✗ Men built the tower of Babel (see Genesis 11:1-9).

✗ Joshua and his soldiers marched around a city (see Joshua 6).

As you look at the above list of tasks, think about the tools in the male internal toolbox and ask yourself which ones you see at work. You can see that during biblical times, men relied on their problem-solving, take-charge, competitive-drive, and task-oriented tools to get things done. They also used their fact-finding and fact-giving tools—but not always with good results.

WHEN FACTS WEREN'T ENOUGH

Picture the following scene from the book of Daniel.

One day the king is going about his kingly tasks when up from the ranks comes a handful of his guys. They have an idea. "We think you need a new decree, King," they tell him.

"Okay." The king blinks. "What is it?"

Now, at this point a woman would have had a hundred questions—many of them having to do with how the new decree will affect others and how it will make them feel: Why do we need a new decree? What about the people? How will they react to a new decree? Don't we have enough decrees? Isn't my kingdom running smoothly? Aren't the people getting along?

But this king, being a man, didn't ask any questions. He just took the facts as his guys presented them, and when they suggested that no one in the kingdom should worship anyone but the king himself for the next thirty days, he had all the facts he needed.

"Sure!" the king said, his take-charge tool kicking in. "Let it be done." And *those* were all the facts the king needed to give.

There you have it—the use of the fact-giving, fact-finding, and take-charge tools in the simplest of ways.

The problem was that the king hadn't considered the likes of Daniel. Daniel wouldn't have dreamed of praying to an earthly king because he had something special going with the one true King.

When the king's guys informed him that Daniel refused to worship anyone but the true and living God, the king took note of that fact and made this pronouncement: "To the lions' den with him! Let his God save him!"

Of course, this story has a happy ending. When Daniel brushed off the lion hair and waltzed out of that dark, dangerous den without so much as a scratch, the king had all the facts he needed to make *another* decision, this one to follow the God of all creation.

TOOL TIP

Almost from the beginning of time, we guys have made use of our natural internal tools to do the things God has for us to do.

This is a biblical picture of typical guy behavior. Here's the king, taking care of tasks, fixing things, and getting and giving facts. When he receives a little information—in this case a suggestion from his guys—he makes a decision without weighing the ramifications.

We guys do much the same today. We give and receive information, then use our other internal tools—the problem-solving, take-charge, competitive-drive, and task-oriented tools—without weighing the relational and emotional ramifications our actions have on those we love.

As we shall discover later in this book, these kinds of decisions require an entirely different set of tools.

GETTING—AND KEEPING—IT ALL GOING

As you read through Scripture, you can see very plainly that God needed a lot of guys to get the human community off the ground. Just think of all the building and developing and problem solving that went on while men constructed cities, built civilizations, and put in roads. Guys had a lot of opportunities to use their internal toolboxes.

God took the man's role in establishing and running his world very seriously. And when a man didn't do the task he was assigned, God doled out some big-time consequences. Jonah and Achan found that out the hard way.

In Jonah's case the consequences were very dark indeed. Jonah didn't care much for the job of warning the folks of Nineveh about their impending doom. So he ran away. The result? He wound up looking at what God wanted from a different light—the dim light of the inside of a fish belly.

Then there was Achan. God gave him a fairly simple job: Take the city but nothing in it. Achan's competitive-drive tool—which was helpful in getting the job done—caused him to pause and think twice about the second half of that decree. *It couldn't hurt to take something for myself,* he figured. *God wouldn't know, and besides, the other guys would probably be impressed if they found out. And hey, it's just a little something. Who would miss it?*

As it turned out, God was serious. Achan buried his stolen treasure, and not long afterward his buddies buried him.

God made use of the tools in a man's internal toolbox for his own purposes. But when men didn't take into account their relationships—particularly their relationships with him—there were consequences.

THE WORLD'S FIRST RELATIONAL TOOLS

While the Bible doesn't come out and say it, our guess is the women in Old Testament times were busy taking care of the relational aspects of developing a society. This is not a sexist stereotype. Women, after all, have generally been blessed with more emotional relational tools than men have. Because of that, women's days probably involved tasks such as:

✗ Nurturing children
✗ Encouraging men about their role at work
✗ Building up the self-esteem of men
✗ Helping men understand the need for relating
✗ Teaching men how to relate to children
✗ Expressing the importance of having a relationship with God

What was true then is still true today: Men and women relate differently, using different relational tools.

We have done quite a lot of research on how men and women adapt to their given roles in the family and in society, and how they develop different internal tools as a result. What we've found is that men and women seem to gravitate naturally toward certain roles. Not surprisingly, men tend to move toward the role of physical provider while women seem to move toward that of emotional provider.

But where did these roles come from, and why does each gender tend to fill one of these specific roles?

The following paragraphs share some of the information we have gathered concerning these roles and the internal tools it takes to fill them.

WHO'S PROVIDING WHAT?

Where did our internal tools come from, anyway? Our research suggests that they came out of necessity, as men and women took on very distinct but overlapping roles within families and society. Early in human history men spent their time providing for the physical needs of their families and protecting them as well; women tended to take care of the family's relational or emotional needs. Because of that, a man's days probably involved tasks such as:

✗ Building a home
✗ Building a village
✗ Making passable trails to and from the village
✗ Preparing for winter
✗ Finding and hunting food

✗ Working the land
✗ Tending to the animals

This is not to say that men are off the hook when it comes to the relational needs of their families or loved ones. And it's not to say that women provide only emotional care for their families. But the simple fact is that over time, men and women have taken on these roles, as demonstrated in the following diagram.

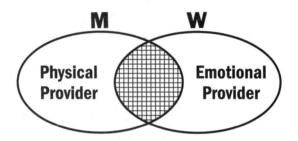

Research and polling from the U.S. Census Bureau agree that, even today, men and women gravitate toward the roles reflected in the diagram. For example, a recent study by the bureau showed a decline in the number of working women with infant children. The rates fell from an all-time high of 59 percent in 1998 to 55 percent in 2000. In 1976 only 31 percent of new mothers were in the workforce, and many experts believe that the statistics are headed back to that level.[1]

But that's not all. Nationwide polls consistently report that women in the workforce would rather stay at home with their children. In 1996 the Independent Women's Forum asked women the following question: "If you had enough money to live as comfortably as you'd like, would you prefer to work full-time, work part-time, do volunteer work, or work at home caring for your family?" Only 15 percent of the respondents said that they wanted to work full-time. The largest percentage said they wanted to be at home with their children.[2]

In addition, a 1997 Pew Research Center poll found that only one-third of mothers with children under age eighteen said they prefer working full-time over working part-time or not at all.[3]

We did some research of our own. In order to understand how people define the terms *physical provider* and *emotional provider,* we surveyed 2,000 seminar attendees. See the chart below for the results.

PHYSICAL PROVIDER	EMOTIONAL PROVIDER
Provides financially or brings home the bulk of the family income	Makes sure the emotional needs of family are met
Makes sure the house and car are in good working order	Creates safe environment for expressing feelings and affection
Does heavy labor—moves heavy things and acts as handyman	Keeps harmony; acts as peacemaker
Guides family; serves as spiritual leader	Listens, encourages, nurtures, comforts, counsels
Provides a safe and secure environment	Keeps records of the heritage

From the beginning of time, men and women have provided for their families. The difference is in what each of them provides. The question remains, how did it come to be that way?

We believe it came as a result of one of God's gifts to humanity: the ability to adapt.

ADAPTING BY DEVELOPING THE PROPER TOOLS

Adaptation involves making changes that help us to excel at the task at hand or under certain conditions. Adaptation has helped humans survive and flourish in all sorts of conditions. For example, the bodies of people who live in colder climates have adapted by storing more fat cells, which provides insulation to keep them warm. On the other hand, the bodies of people who live closer to the equator, where the temperature is warmer and the sun shines more, have adapted over the centuries by producing chemicals that cause darker skin pigmentation, which protects them from damaging sun rays.

If you want a short-term example of adaptation, think about what happens when you go barefoot for long periods of time or if you use your hands for hard manual labor. That's right—you grow calluses.

GUY FACT

The divorce rate is low among marriages in which the husband earns most of the family income.

Just as God has given our bodies the ability to adapt, he also has designed our emotional makeup with the ability to adapt.

In biblical times people adapted to their God-ordained roles. Since it was the man's role to provide physically, God equipped him to handle that as his primary task. And since it was the woman's role to provide emotional support for her family, God equipped her to do just that.

This is not to say that many men aren't naturally equipped for relationships. In fact, many guys are gifted in this area. They possess the internal tools that aid them in their personal relationships. Conversely, it also doesn't mean a woman can't be gifted at business or in providing for the physical needs of her family. Many women truly are "wired" to provide for their families in that way. This all simply means that history—biblical and otherwise—shows us why most guys could stand to add a few relational tools to their internal toolboxes.

Over the centuries the focus of guys has changed so that men can now concern themselves more with meeting the emotional needs of their loved ones. But what was the focus of those early guys? Let's take a look.

A MATTER OF FOCUS

If you think *you* need to add some relational tools to your internal toolbox, then just take a look at the guys who lived at the beginning of history. They didn't even have time to think about relational tools, let alone do anything with them.

These early guys were focused on providing and protecting, which included tasks such as building homes and villages, making passable trails, preparing for winter, gathering and hunting food, working the land, and tending to their animals. At that time in history and in that culture, men very likely didn't have time to focus on how well they communicated with their loved ones, on spending quality time with those they loved, or on their family's relational needs.

In other words, the early guys adapted to their situations and their roles by becoming adept at developing and using the tools necessary to be effective providers and protectors. Men back then couldn't afford to sit around talking about relationships. Not when they had wheels to invent, villages to build, and a society to pull together. Had they thought more about relationships, then we might not have some of the struggles between men and women that we have today. We also can't help but think that if they'd spent their time on those things, society might not have gotten off the ground.

GUY FACT

The average person laughs thirteen times a day.

Today it seems that men have to adapt all over again.

THE DIFFERENT ROLES OF MEN AND WOMEN

According to the Society for Neuroscience, in ancient times each sex had a very defined role that helped ensure the survival of the species. Men hunted. Women gathered food near the home and cared for the children. Different areas of their brains may have been sharpened to enable each sex to carry out their jobs. Professor David Geary at the University of Missouri, a researcher in the area of gender differences, thinks that developing superior navigation skills may have enabled men to become better suited to the role of hunter, while developing a preference for landmarks may have enabled women to fulfill the task of gathering food closer to home.[4]

When we consider the fact that men have for the most part adapted to the role of physical provider while women have adapted to the role of emotional provider, it's no wonder we guys struggle in our relationships with women. Both of these roles require specific skills—specific tools—that men and women have developed since biblical times, and in too many cases, men and women are either physical pro-viders or emotional providers, with very little in between.

The problem in many of our relationships is this: Often the degree to which a person lives and operates either as a physical provider or as an emotional provider is the degree to which he or she lacks the oppo-site tools. In other words, if a man is on the extreme end of being a physical provider, then he will likely develop the specific tools that al-low him to be successful as a physical provider; however, he may lack the tools it takes to be a good emotional provider.

This problem is reflected in many of our surveys.

PROVIDER TOOLS—AN EXTREME LOOK

We surveyed hundreds of people at our seminars and asked them what they believe can happen to men who are on the extreme end of being a physical provider. Here are some of the answers we received:

✗ They may spend more time at work than at home, and the family may feel neglected.
✗ They may become passive in their relationships, unplugged emotionally and spiritually.
✗ If they are the exclusive wage earner, they may not feel the need to help with household chores.
✗ They may become too busy to parent, too busy to be available for their family's emotional needs.

Michael knows that staying away from the extreme can be a struggle. He says, "I sometimes feel an incredible pull toward spending more time providing for my family through work than providing for them through emotional ways. What I realized, however, is that my pull to provide through work is really a drive to be accomplished, to suc-ceed, rather than a drive to provide for my family. Realizing this has helped me gain a more realistic picture of why I would rather work than hang out at home. I don't beat myself down because of these feelings. I believe they come from hundreds of generations of men who felt forced to work rather than help out at home. When I do feel the pull to be significant at work rather than at home, I remind myself that when I am on my deathbed, the last thing on my mind will be what I accomplished at work. The most important thing to me then will be my family and those I love."

Men are not the only ones drawn to the extremes. Our surveys found that something similar holds true for women who are on the far end of being emotional providers. In other words, the more completely focused they are on being successful emotional providers, the less skilled they often are at being physical providers.

Darcy was such a woman. She focused all her attention on raising her three children. She was incredibly gifted at listening to her children's problems and helping them share their feelings. But when her children were in their early teens, her husband died of cancer. Darcy was suddenly paralyzed by fear of the

GUY FACT

Men have a difficult time relating their own feelings and may feel threatened when others express their feelings. This may cause men to react by withdrawing or attempting to control the situation.

workplace. Why? Because she had focused all her energy on being an emotional provider, and she had few of the tools needed to provide physically for her family.

Obviously, there are problems with either extreme.

So what's the answer?

It's simple, really, especially for us guys. We need to acquire the tools that don't come naturally for us—relational tools. That way we will have not only the tools that make us good protectors and providers but also the tools that can help us enjoy incredible relationships.

Before we get to that, let's take a look at the driving force in all men. It's the hormone that controls many of our thoughts and actions and that sends us scurrying to the far end of the tools continuum. It's the reason we sat around the campfire talking about survival in the first place.

That's right, it's the *T* word.

Testosterone:
Why Guys Are Good
at Being Guys

So far we've looked at why men tend toward functional, provisionary internal tools. We've talked about how ancient men developed those tools as they adapted to the task of building a society and caring for their families. But none of that changes one very important truth: God designed us for relationships.

In Genesis 1:27 we read that God created us in his own image. That means, among other things, that we are relational beings. Later God explains our ultimate relational purpose when he says, "You must worship no other gods, but only the Lord, for he is a God who is passionate about his relationship with you" (Exodus 34:14, NLT).

God even spells out his reason for the marriage relationship. "It is not good for the man to be alone. I will make a helper suitable for him." Then he creates woman (see Genesis 2:18).

So if God created us to be in relationship with him and with others, and if we are created in his image, why is it so difficult for us guys to relate to women? Why do men and women seem so different when it comes to relating and communicating?

Any discussion about the differences between men and women will eventually make its way to the subject of testosterone. Or, as we'll call it in this chapter, the Big T.

Testosterone is the reason we guys have the God-given internal tools we touched on in the last chapter. Much of the evidence on the subject today suggests that a man's personality and behavioral tendencies are shaped by physiological means. More simply put, testosterone affects everything we men do.

That all starts long before we are aware of it.

WHEN GUYS *REALLY* START TO BE LIKE GUYS

A miraculous occurrence takes place in the brain of an unborn baby between the fifth and seventh week in the mother's womb. Until this point baby girl brains are very much like baby boy brains. But between that fifth and seventh week something like a faucet turns on inside both male and female babies, dripping microscopic amounts of testosterone onto their brains. The girls' brains usually get a few drops here and there, but the boys' brains get fairly soaked in the stuff. This causes vast differences in the male or female tendencies of that person.[1]

GUY FACT

In South America it would be rude not to ask a man about his wife, and in most Arab countries it would be rude to do so.

In other words, our internal toolboxes are developed long before we are born.

We now know that certain types of experiences a mother goes through after conception—especially between that fifth and seventh week after conception—can affect the amount of testosterone that washes over a male or female baby's brain. If a mother suffers severe trauma or stress during her pregnancy, it is possible for her body to secrete a hormone that blocks the release of testosterone. As a result, some males have a more "female" brain—they may be less aggressive, more sensitive, and more nurturing.[2]

The amount of Big T that washes over an unborn baby's brain determines—at least in part—a child's personality as an adult. In other words, a baby with a testosterone-soaked brain is more likely to become dominating, factual, self-focused, demanding, and active. A baby whose brain was not flooded by the Big T is more likely to become nurturing, affectionate, gentle, emotional, and generous.

In their book *Brain Sex: The Real Difference between Men and Women,* Anne Moir and David Jessel offer readers a test to determine "maleness" and "femaleness."[3] The test is scored on a scale from -100 (the far end of maleness) to +100 (the far end of femaleness). Our entire staff at the Smalley Relationship Center took the test, and the results were somewhat surprising. Greg scored at the far end of maleness with -80, and Michael scored high on the female side with +80. You can imagine some of the teasing that has gone on in our office! But seriously, the test proved our point that some men are more assertive and competitive while others are more nurturing and compassionate.

HIGH TESTOSTERONE AND THE WIN-AT-ALL-COSTS MENTALITY

When it comes to recreational or work-related activities, the higher a man's testosterone level, the more competitive and solution-oriented he tends to be.

Remember the competitive-drive tool? What do you think is at the bottom of that internal tool? Yep, you guessed it—testosterone! There is a direct relationship between a high testosterone level and a high level of competitiveness in a man.

It is possible to measure the testosterone level in the human brain. A brain with a Big T level above 300 is considered pretty well testosterone flooded. Believe it or not, levels can go as high as 1000. A man whose brain has that level of testosterone is usually off-the-charts competitive.

Check out these examples of a man's desire to win based on where he falls in the following testosterone chart.[4]

TASK	300 T LEVEL	500 T LEVEL	1000 T LEVEL
Sports	Winning makes it fun	Winning is crucial	Can't carry on a conversation for five hours after losing
Chores	Take-charge attitude	Must organize and conquer	Attacks like a warrior
Work	Driven to excel	Being the best matters	No rest until he takes over the company

Men, here's some news for you—a doctor can test your blood or saliva and determine your level of testosterone. But our guess is that whatever your testosterone level is, it won't surprise you. After all, you're the one who spends many hours of your week driven by the Big T.

Now let's take a look at how the Big T affects us men when it comes to our relationships.

A CHIP OFF THE OLD BLOCK

If you are like most men, then the fact that the Big T permeates your brain will affect a host of real-life situations. Testosterone can affect our communication, how we approach intimacy, the recreational activities we choose, our behavior and tendencies, and, of course, our relational skills.

As you look at the above list, you probably will notice that most of the items deal with relationships. The bottom line? Testosterone—and all of us guys have it—affects our ability to relate. And it has probably done that since the time we were little boys.

If you've fretted about your relationships for long, you're probably convinced that sometime around your high school days you made a left turn when you should have gone right. You may feel you stumbled into the quicksand of poor relating and have never found a way to pull yourself out.

If that's you, we've got good news: Things aren't nearly as bad as you think.

And you aren't alone, either.

The internal tools most of us guys use so naturally, the same ones we developed as boys, are simply not the right tools for building relationships. But they are good tools all the same, tools fueled by testosterone.

In fact, we can see the Big T at work in boys almost as soon as they're able to walk. One research study we refer to in our seminar sessions placed small microphones on the shirts or dresses of a group of young children. The tape recorder caught every sound they made for an extended period of time. If you understand this study on testosterone, the results will certainly not surprise you.

GUY FACT
A toothpick is the object most often choked on by Americans.

According to the study, 100 percent of the noises made by little girls were for the purpose of verbal communication. In other words, they used real words to convey real thoughts or questions to themselves or to other children.

However, only 60 percent of the boys' noises were made with the intention of communicating through words. The other 40 percent of their sounds were, well, just sounds. According to the research, here are some of the typical noises the children made:

Girl Noises
✗ "Hi Susie . . ."
✗ "How are you?"
✗ "I got a new dress."
✗ "I'm happy today."
✗ "Isn't teacher pretty?"
✗ "What are we doing with the crayons?"
✗ "I like your lunch box."
✗ "Wanna play with me?"
✗ "Wanna talk?"

Boy Noises

✗ *"Swishhhhhhh . . . Swishhhhhhh . . . "* (the sound of a sword)
✗ *"Rerrerrerrerrerrer . . . "* (the sound of a truck)
✗ *"Shhhhhhhhhhhhhhhoooo . . . "* (the sound of an airplane)
✗ *"P'kew, p'kew, p'kew . . . tatatatata . . . ."* (the sound of a gun)
✗ *"Rurrrrrrrrrrrrr . . . . Rurrrrrrrrrrrrr . . . "* (the sound of a siren)
✗ *"Ruf, ruf . . . Ooooohooooohooooooo . . . "* (the sounds of animals)
✗ *"Ughhhhhhh!"* (screaming sounds)
✗ *"Ahhhhhhh . . . ha-ha-ha-ha"* (shouting sounds, laughing)

Now, we guys know that those boy sounds actually *are* a form of verbal communication. But what they communicate are statements such as, "I'm the biggest truck, so get out of my way."

In addition to the nonverbal sounds the boys used to communicate, they also used boys' typical verbal communication. We found that in 60 percent of the noises that actually involved words, the communication was almost entirely functional or factual:

✗ "What's in your lunch?"
✗ "It's recess time."
✗ "I'm bigger than you."
✗ "Let's go!"
✗ "Give me that truck."
✗ "I can beat you to the fence."

What does this list show us? An identical picture of what goes on with guys in the workplace—guys who might lack a few relational tools when they come home at the end of the day.

Remember our list of God-given internal tools? Let's look at the list of things boys say to each other, then match those statements with the internal tools most men rely on. We'll see that those male internal tools are already at work in young boys:

BOYS' CONVERSATION	TOOL USED
"What's in your lunch?"	Fact-finding tool
"It's recess time."	Fact-giving tool
"I'm bigger than you."	Take-charge tool
"Let's go!"	Task-oriented tool
"Give me that truck."	Problem-solving tool
"I can beat you to the fence."	Competitive-drive tool

We've found this same phenomenon at work in adult men everywhere we go. It's no wonder to us, then, that men have such a difficult time communicating with women.

If you struggle with relating to women, testosterone likely has something to do with it. The reason for this should be obvious—the male brain and the female brain are different, and a lot of the difference traces back to the level of testosterone.

Testosterone keeps men from communicating and relating as well as women do. It also causes us to unconsciously keep what we call a daily word count.

TESTOSTERONE AND A MAN'S DAILY WORD COUNT

If you've spent any time arguing with a woman about your "inability to talk about things," then the following fact probably won't surprise you: On the average, a man's daily word count is less than half of a woman's. Women speak an average of 30,000 words a day while men speak about 12,000. In fact, the higher a man's testosterone level, the lower his daily word count tends to be.

We all know that men use fewer words than women do, and most of us use our "allotment of words" at work. Remember, lots of us men are aggressive and driven, and we'll talk at length in the workplace in order to successfully complete an assignment, project, or task. Here are a few ways guys gobble up their brain's average daily word count at work: giving instructions to other employees and input to coworkers, talking to customers or clients about a specific product or purchase, gaining instructions from their boss, and explaining a facet of their job to coworkers or clients.

A woman, on the other hand, averages many more spoken words a day than a man does. And the words a woman uses aren't just any words; her words have an impact on her heart and the hearts of the people around her. When a woman spends her day in the workplace, she often has fewer opportunities to use her allotment of words. Many women will compensate in the following ways: lengthy conversations with other women, phone calls to friends (sometimes describing for upwards of an hour the details of a single event), telling stories to children, and recapping what she has read or heard on television.

GUY FACT

Men often assume that giving advice and fixing problems are the best ways to show love; women often just want someone to listen to them.

Here's the problem. At the end of the day—whether the woman works in an office or in the home—there is a huge difference between the number of words the man has left for the day and the number the woman has left.

By the end of the workday, men have spent nearly all their words. We come home for the most part tired and drained, looking for a place to recharge for the next day's battle at the office. Most women, however, are just warming up. They have thousands of words left to speak. And since our word count is depleted, the conversations often turn into unemotional question-and-answer sessions that sound something like this:

"How are you?" she asks.
"Fine," he utters, occasionally making eye contact.
She tries again. "How was work?"
"Good."
Suddenly the ball is rolling in a way he feels helpless to stop, even though he knows with utmost certainty that when it does stop, he'll somehow be underneath it.

"Okay," she sighs. "Anything different or unusual happen?"

"Nope."

"Any interesting conversations with anyone?"

"No."

"Did you get that project finished, the one you were working on yesterday?"

"Yes."

"How did it go?"

"Great."

She studies his eyes. "You seem a little tired. Did anything bad happen?"

"No. Nothing."

"But you're not excited. I mean, I thought you'd be happy to see me. I've been looking forward to talking to you all day, and you don't seem to have anything to say. Are you upset with me or something?"

"No, not at all."

"Are you listening to me?"

"Yes, I'm listening."

Now her tone is less friendly. "You know," she says, "it doesn't feel as if you're really listening to me. I wait all day to talk to you, and this is what I get. Just a couple of one-word answers."

(Pause)

"See. You have nothing to say. How am I supposed to believe you love me when you can't even *talk* to me?"

(Pause)

"Fine. I'm going upstairs. I'll be there if you decide you want to talk."

"Okay."

If you've ever been in a situation like this one, go ahead and smile. We're pretty sure you can relate to the scene above, but we're just as sure that there's hope for your situation. A little later in the book we'll

> ## GUY FACT
> According to studies conducted at Northwestern University, men change their minds two to three times more often than women do.

talk at length about how the fact-finding and fact-giving tools don't work well when it comes to building an open relationship with a woman. And we'll also talk about the internal tools you can acquire and learn to use so that you can overcome your testosterone-caused reluctance to talk—really talk—with those you love.

But before we do that, let's take a look at a few other relational tools—the ones that make it easy for guys to relate to guys.

Tools That Help Guys Relate to Guys

Ever wonder why guys have a fairly easy time relating to one another? We believe it's because most of us have a good grip on a handful of special relational tools—tools that help guys relate to guys.

These very special relational tools have an amazing ability to help us guys create treasured memories that come to mind far more often and far more vividly than, say, our anniversary dates or our kids' birthdays. These are tools that help men not only relate to one another but also bond together.

This is not to say we guys don't struggle in our relationships with one another. For example, we know dozens of men who loved and admired their fathers but never found a way to tell them so to their faces. The simple truth is this: Male bonding does not always require emotionally laden words or in-depth communication. Why? Because most men approach life with the same internal tools. We don't need an open-sharing moment when giving facts will suffice. As comedian Dennis Swanberg put it, when his father wanted to tell Dennis he loved him, he would say, "Want to drive my pickup?"

The real reason we men get along so well together is that in addition to the internal tools we've already mentioned earlier in this book, we have these other tools—specialized tools that help us relate well with each other. We've talked to hundreds of guys in an effort to figure out what those tools are and how they're used.

GUY FACT

Women's sense of self is defined through their feelings and the quality of their relationships. They spend much time supporting, nurturing, and helping each other. They experience fulfillment through sharing and relating.

Before we move on to the relational tools that can help us build strong bonds with those we love, let's take a look at the reason guys get along so well with each other. Or as TV character Hayden Fox once said: "Let's go to Men's Town."

We want to start with a relational tool we guys often use, even if we don't think of it in terms of being a relational tool. It is what we will call the stupid-humor tool.

THE STUPID-HUMOR TOOL

Something about the emotional and mental makeup of a guy makes it easy for him to bond with someone who makes him laugh, who shares his view of what is really funny.

Guys like to laugh, but more than that, they like to laugh when they are together. In general, guys enjoy laughing at jokes (lightbulb jokes, why-did-the-chicken-cross-the-road jokes, relationship jokes), spoof-type movies (*Blazing Saddles, Pink Panther* movies, *Airplane!, The Naked Gun,* and *This Is Spinal Tap,* for example), and slapstick humor (the Three Stooges).

Michael tells the story of a seminar he led one weekend in Texas. His longtime friend Jason, a pilot, flew Michael to the city and stayed with him for the weekend. Now, you might think that a master's-level trained therapist would prepare for the seminar by staying focused on the theme of the meetings, but not Michael. He and Jason went out and watched *Kung Pow: Enter the Fist*—a spoof of a 1970s Bruce Lee movie. Talk about stupid humor. They laughed so hard at this movie that at the end, their eyes were red from their howling. The voice-overs were hilarious, as if the writer tried to write the script to mimic the Asian actors' mouth movements. So the dialogue made no sense at all, and as for the plot, that was thrown out before the script was written! Not only did Jason and Michael bond, but the humor relaxed Michael and got him ready for teaching the seminar.

Laughter is almost always a huge part in most lasting relationships between guys. For most women, laughter is a great bonus, but for the majority of us guys, it's a must. Here's an example of what we're talking about.

Steve, Phil, and Shawn were looking for something to do one Saturday night. While they sat around the table at their favorite Chinese restaurant, sipping tea and waiting for their food order, Phil scanned the entertainment section of the local Saturday paper. That's when it caught his eye: a tiny advertisement for a special event at one of the local mom-and-pop movie theaters, the kind we all visited when we were kids, the kind you can't find anywhere now, except in the smallest of the small towns.

GUY FACT

Apples are more efficient than caffeine in keeping people awake in the mornings.

Phil saw what would be taking place that very night, and without even asking himself if it would appeal to his two friends, he announced their plans for the rest of the evening. "Guys!" he blurted out as the waitress served up orders of Kung Pao chicken, Hunan beef, and sesame pork (all cooked extra spicy, just the way guys like it). "At midnight tonight the Bijou Theatre is having a Three Stooges festival!"

All three of these young men had seen every Three Stooges short ever made—including the ones with Shemp. But this was on the big screen, late at night.

And they would be together.

That night Steve, Phil, and Shawn were primed for the Stooges. They were, as one of them said, "in rare form" as they continued their evening together, laughing at Steve's jokes, Phil's clumsiness, and Shawn's fearlessness when it comes to intentionally making a fool of himself in public. These guys laughed to the point of pain as they watched three grown men clobber, poke, trip, and belittle one another in one short feature after another. *Oh! A wise guy, huh? Nyuk! Nyuk!*

Steve would later marvel at how much funnier the Three Stooges were at one o'clock in the morning, when he and his two friends were just tired enough to laugh at anything. For years to come, these three guys would remember that night as the night they laughed so hard for so long that their chests ached as they headed out of the Bijou and into the night air.

That would also be a night when these three guys bonded in a way that only guys can bond—through laughter.

As important a relational tool as laughter is in the bonding process between men, two more tools bring men just as close. The first of these is what we'll call the shared-experience tool.

THE SHARED-EXPERIENCE TOOL

While women feel closer and validated through communication, dialogue, and intimate sharing, many men tend to find such sharing and involvement uncomfortable, if not overwhelming. Men feel closer and validated through shared activities such as sports, competition, and outdoor activities.

A lot of guys look back on shared experiences—whether they be funny, adventurous, or frightening—much the same way many women look at anniversaries with the man they love—first dates, engagements, and, of course, weddings.

The kind of experience that bonds most guys generally doesn't take place in a formal manner. In fact, many times shared experiences between the guys we know wind up involving rescue maneuvers and quite often medical intervention. See if you and your friends can relate to any of the following stories.

Bob, a good friend of ours, enjoyed a special shared experience with some of his buddies back when he was in high school. Today Bob is a respected marketing executive who still enjoys a good adventure. But none will ever compare to the adventure he had as a high school junior.

Bob was a lineman on the school's football team, and it was Friday night, hours after the biggest game of the season. Bob and a few of his buddies decided to meet at the local park to swap war stories from the gridiron and to engage in general silliness—standing in moving pickup trucks, doing doughnuts, and packing seven guys into a Volkswagen—you know, the kind of silliness that Bob now warns his own son against.

About thirty minutes into the get-together, Bob and his friends decided they were hot. It was September and unseasonably warm. It was time to find a place to go for a swim.

"Look at that," one of Bob's friends said. "A pool!"

And sure enough. There across the parking lot, thirty yards into the park grounds, was a pool the city engineers had built that summer. It was long and wide, and from their place in the pitch-dark parking lot, it looked tempting.

GUY FACT

The average iceberg weighs 20,000,000 tons.

Too tempting to pass up.

"Let's go!" one of Bob's buddies called out as he waved at the others.

"Yeah!"

"Great idea!"

En masse they headed for the pool. But Bob and his friends soon discovered one problem. The pool was completely surrounded by eight-foot-tall fencing and two very well-locked gates. Bob and the others looked at each other.

"Cool," one said.

"So cool," another added.

Which meant that an adventure such as swimming in a closed park pool late at night could only be made better if it also involved scaling an eight-foot fence. The guys had a quick discussion and decided that only one or two of them should go first. The others, they thought, would keep a lookout in case someone official, say, a police officer, did not find this particular outdoor adventure either cool or legal.

The boys chose Bob and a buddy as the first climbers.

In the same way Bob once tackled opposing linemen, he sized up the fence and attacked it full force. He was over and onto the cement decking in four seconds flat.

Bob's friends shouted their approval with a variety of grunts and hoots.

In another few seconds Bob stripped down to his underwear, ran full bore up and onto the diving board, jumped three solid times, and hopped in feet first.

That's when he realized the next problem.

The pool was empty. Dry as a bone. Less water than the parking-lot puddles.

Instead of making a splash, Bob's body sailed silently into the pool and landed with a sickening thud somewhere near the deep end.

"Ughhh," Bob moaned.

Now, this type of adventure would have killed or crippled a grown man. But it takes more than jumping into an empty park pool late one Friday night to permanently damage a teenage boy bent on adventure.

In this case Bob's buddies realized a couple things right off. First, Bob was hurt—maybe badly. Second, Bob couldn't get out of the pool. Third, Bob weighed just under three hundred pounds, and none of them could carry him over the fence.

This was before people had cell phones, so calling for help was—for the time being—out of the question.

"I have a towrope!" one of them shouted.

In what became a very memorable secondary adventure, Bob's

GUY FACT

According to the *Farmers' Almanac* a couple can test their love by placing two acorns in water. If the acorns float together, their love is true; if they drift apart, so will the man and woman.

buddies drove a truck onto the park grass and up to the closest gate. There they hooked the towrope to the latch and, using a great deal of engine power, pulled the gate from its hinges.

"Ughhh!" Bob moaned, a bit quieter this time.

"We're coming, dude. Hang on!"

Bob's buddies trotted down the pool steps, then scampered along the shallow area and into the deep end.

"I don't think we should lift him," one of the guys pointed out. "His neck could be broken."

"Bob?" another teenager called as he stepped forward. "Are you breathing?" The boy squinted at Bob, a nearly naked, moaning blob lying in the shadows of a dark, empty swimming pool.

GUY FACT

American Airlines saved $40,000 in 1987 by eliminating one olive from each salad served in first class.

"Ughhh," was Bob's answer.

And in that way they determined that Bob's neck was not broken. Gathering around all sides of him, they carried Bob up and out of the pool, across the deck, and into the back of the pickup truck.

Ten minutes later they were explaining the situation to the emergency-room doctor at the nearest hospital.

As it turned out, Bob had broken both his legs. *Shattered* was the word the doctor used, actually. Bob had to have reconstructive surgery on his knees and hips and was in a full-body cast through Christmas.

"The amazing thing," Bob notes today, "is that none of us drank a single beer that night. The doctor thought we must've been drunk, but that wasn't it at all. We just wanted to have a good time."

It is this type of experience that bonds guys and makes their eyes mist up twenty years later at a high school reunion.

"We sure had a good time, didn't we?" one will ask the other.

"Unforgettable," another will add.

And the thing that every one of you men will understand is this— even twenty years later, these men will mean every word when they reminisce about that night. The memories of that wild experience will far outweigh the fact that Bob's legs will forever ache when the temperature drops below sixty.

That's how the shared-experience tool works.

THE OUTDOOR-ADVENTURE TOOL

Men were made for adventure—particularly outdoor adventure. Lots of guys tell stories of the fish they caught, the deer they bagged, or the mountain they climbed. It's part of being a guy, and it's also part of bonding with other guys.

If you don't believe that, take a trip to your local magazine rack and look at the publications that deal with outdoor adventures. You'll see magazines for every conceivable outdoor activity—hunting, fishing, hiking, and stunt cycling, to name a few.

We've known a lot of men who enjoy outdoor adventures and who have bonded with one another through those adventures. Here's the story of Sean, who shared an unforgettable outdoor adventure with his friends.

Sean and his wife have struggled for ten years with communication, sensitivity, and tenderness. Sean is currently learning new tools that will help him bond with his wife. He needed no help, however, bonding with his male friends.

Sean and his friends are doctors who live and practice in Portland, Oregon. One is a surgeon and the others specialize in varying types of medicine. Combined, they have acquired several decades of training and education.

When Sean and the guys have a day off, their favorite way to spend it is with Betsy—Sean's sorry-looking red boat with chipped paint and a sputtering outboard motor. Betsy's motor sometimes has a mind of its own, turning over with the same reluctance as a netted fish.

For Sean and his buddies, there is nothing like a day on the water.

One day a few summers ago, the guys were itching for some outdoor adventure. Over breakfast they planned a trip for the next week.

"Let's fish in the river," Sean said.

"The Lewis, you mean?" The eyes of every guy were immediately wide with anticipation. The Lewis River is fairly calm and known for its many fishing spots.

"No . . . let's get a little crazy," Sean said. He could almost feel the wind on his face, the rod in his hands. "I'm thinking about the Columbia."

The Columbia River is as similar to the Lewis as a salmon is to a minnow. The Columbia is a full-size channel traversed by barges and other freight-bearing ships. The current is swift, the water deep and icy cold.

But the cold, deep water of the Columbia means one thing for certain: fish. Big fish. Sean and his buddies had never fished this particular river—mostly, they said later, because their wives wouldn't let them. Their wives knew that every year people on fishing trips drown in the Columbia, and—as their wives put it—fish simply aren't worth the risk.

> **GUY FACT**
> A giraffe can clean its ears with its twenty-one-inch tongue.

But that isn't always true for everyone. Especially for a group of guys antsy for some outdoor adventure. That morning all four doctors began talking at once, agreeing unanimously that the following week they'd fish the Columbia.

When they pulled out from the docks the next Wednesday, Sean had another idea. "Let's take the middle of the river. I heard the fish are amazing out there."

"Great!" his companions responded.

With that, they motored out to the middle of the Columbia River for a little outdoor adventure. Decades of graduate course work didn't elicit even a single warning light on the panels of these four doctors' minds.

The current was strong that day, and they hadn't remembered to bring an anchor, so Sean put one man at a time in charge of keeping the boat in place. That man situated himself facing the rear of the boat where he could monitor Betsy's continual engine output, giving her a burst of power now and then when she threatened to drift too far off course.

That left three men to do the most important job—bait the hooks and fish. To keep things fair, the four of them took turns working Betsy's motor.

As it turned out, the fish were biting madly that day. One after another, the men reeled in fish until they had a string of salmon like none they'd ever seen before. They would have kept fishing until dusk had they not heard a sudden and violent horn.

Hoonnk!

"This was not your average horn," Sean pointed out later. "This was the kind of horn that passed through your body and took your heart with it. It was louder than a train."

Only then did all four doctors look up to see the ship bearing down on them forty or fifty yards away. Many times an unforgettable male-type outdoor adventure requires fast thinking. This was certainly the case for Sean and his friends.

In a matter of seconds they made several pertinent observations. First they observed that they were about to be overtaken by several hundred tons of steel, in which case their bodies would probably never be found—and no one would ever know about the fish they'd caught that day.

Second, since swimming wasn't an outdoor adventure they'd practiced since their teenage years, they needed life jackets. At the bow of the boat there were four Mickey Mouse life vests belonging to Sean's children.

"Grab a jacket!" Sean shouted.

Each of the doctors grabbed a Mickey Mouse life vest and slipped it around his neck. Sean gave Betsy full throttle, at which point her engine sputtered and summarily died.

"Jump!" Sean yelled, and at that instant, the ship laid on its horn once more.

> **GUY FACT**
>
> In India it is perfectly proper for men to wear pajamas in public. Pajamas are accepted as standard daytime wearing apparel.

Hoonnk!

All four men jumped into the icy Columbia and began swimming for their lives toward the distant shore. Fortunately, a Coast Guard boat—traveling not far away—spotted the trouble and headed immediately in their direction.

Sean and his doctor friends swam—cartoon style—at what felt like fifty miles per hour toward the rescue boat. They were snatched from certain death just as the ship passed by, towering over them like a skyscraper. Sean watched Betsy crumble into kindling as the ship mowed her down.

"It was awesome," Sean says now. "The power of it all."

Sean and his friends were in the water just five minutes, but each of the four was shaking like an off-balance washing machine.

"You could've been killed," the Coast Guard officer observed. Sean remembered later that the man didn't sound angry, just factual. He was a guy, after all, and could probably relate to the adventure on many levels.

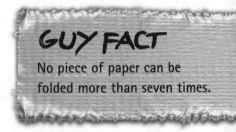

GUY FACT
No piece of paper can be folded more than seven times.

"We w-w-w-wanted the b-b-b-big f-f-fish," Sean explained, his teeth chattering madly. The Coast Guard officer informed him that the center of the channel is reserved for large ocean liners and freight-bearing ships.

"Oh," was all Sean could manage.

The story had a happy ending. The frozen doctors had to spend only two hours at the hospital while their colleagues gathered around them, telling jokes and working to raise their body temperatures to a safe level.

Also—and this is classic guy behavior—one of Sean's friends had managed to grab the string of valuable salmon as he jumped into the Columbia. In the emergency room, before reaching for a stack of warm blankets for Sean and his friends, a doctor on staff took the fish, placed them in a clean bucket, and covered them with ice.

First things first, you know.

So the trip was not a total loss, even though the resulting discussion between Sean and his wife sent them both to counseling.

And best of all, it created a type of outdoor adventure that Sean continues to share with his friends and will share with his children and grandchildren for decades to come.

Sean's story is like that of many guys who have had their own outdoor adventures. Most men probably haven't faced the kind of danger he faced that day on the Columbia River. But the outdoor adventures they share with other guys bond them with those friends.

Gary learned that firsthand in a most memorable outdoor adventure. We'll let him tell the story.

GARY'S OUTDOOR ADVENTURE

Not long ago I was at a dinner party where a friend of mine—I'll call him Junior—talked at length about his outdoor adventures hunting turkey. He talked of the brown and green camouflage clothing he wore, the weight of the gun on his shoulder as he tiptoed through the brush, the release of adrenaline when he spotted a turkey, and the sense of adventure that came from felling it, bagging it, and taking it home for dinner.

> **GUY FACT**
>
> One cow is enough to make 400 quarter-pounder sandwiches.

I was sixty-one years old with a busy schedule that included a dozen meetings, taped interviews, and speaking engagements. But the idea of that type of outdoor adventure was more than I could pass up.

Junior and I made a plan, and that spring we took to the Ozark Mountains, dressed, armed, and ready for adventure. He drove, leading us up winding forest roads deep into the backwoods of the Ozarks. When we'd reached the end of a narrow dirt road, he looked at me and grinned. "Now we foot it!"

"Great!" I grabbed my gear and my gun, and the two of us headed out.

We began walking. Up and up we went, moving as quietly as possible and searching the brush for any sign of movement. Some three

hundred yards up the hill, through bramble and bushes and dense vege-
tation, we heard what sounded like a turkey. A few seconds passed, and
suddenly . . . there it was. The largest, grandest wild tom I'd ever seen.

"The first one's yours." Junior nodded at me.

At about that time I began to feel chest pains.

In the back of my mind I recalled that both my father and brother
had died of heart attacks before their sixtieth birthdays. In fact, I was
the first Smalley man to survive beyond age sixty without having a
heart attack. Also, Junior and I were a
good fifteen miles from the nearest
paved road and an hour from any medical facility.

But all of these details were only
momentary news flashes in the control
center of my brain. The important thing
was this: I had my first wild turkey in
firing range! My outdoor adventure was just getting good, which meant
my chest pains would have to wait.

GUY FACT

Men laugh longer, more loudly,
and more often than women.

"Okay, be real still." Junior crouched down beside me, slow and
deliberate. "Get the bird in your viewfinder."

I raised the gun, and the pain in my chest ratcheted up. "I've got
it!" I whispered, not so much because of the turkey but because I
couldn't find my voice.

"Shoot!" Junior hissed.

The pain tripled when I pulled the trigger. As the turkey fell to the
ground, so did I.

In typical guy fashion, Junior did not notice that I was lying in a
heap amidst the leaves and shrubs. He ran for the turkey, grabbed it by the
feet, and carried it back to me. "It's huge!" he announced. "Way to go!"

So the outdoor adventure would've been perfect except I was
pretty much paralyzed on the ground in the middle of what I was fairly
certain was a full-blown heart attack. "I'm . . . having . . . a heart attack." I gasped the words, using all my strength to make them loud
enough for Junior to hear.

"Very funny," Junior shot back. He thought I was kidding, and he waved the turkey at me and said, "Look at this thing, will ya? That's a great bird for your first shot, Gary."

"Junior . . . " my strength was waning, though a part of me was deeply proud of the turkey. "I'm serious. I'm . . . it's bad, Junior. I can't walk."

Though I'm often the cutup in a group setting, Junior suddenly realized I was telling the truth. He snapped into action, recognizing that we had just launched into an altogether different type of outdoor adventure.

"You can't walk? Really?" Junior's face was pale now. He rubbed the palms of his hands on his camouflaged hunting pants. "I'll go call for help—don't go anywhere."

No danger of that.

Junior swung the turkey over his back and made off through the brush. Now remember, we were at least three football fields away from our car when this happened. From my spot on the ground, I watched Junior and the turkey leave, and there I was, my face smashed against the damp sod, curled in a ball, struggling for every breath.

A fly landed on my nose, but I didn't have the strength to brush it off. I pictured other turkeys—or bobcats for that matter—circling me, pecking at me, nibbling at my arms and legs in a kind of outdoor adventure I had never anticipated. They could have done whatever they wanted to me because I was too weak to move, too weak to care.

Thoughts raced through my mind. Thoughts that aren't entirely unheard of for a man in the midst of an outdoor adventure. *Okay, God . . . if this is it, thanks for such a great life. . . . Thanks for my family. . . . Let them know how much I love them. . . . Let me live long enough to tell them good-bye. . . .*

Finally Junior returned, huffing and looking alarmed. "The paramedics are coming! We have to meet them down the road." Sweat beaded up on his forehead. "They aren't sure about this area."

That left us one option.

Junior picked me up much the way he'd picked up the wild turkey.

He heaved me over his shoulders and draped my body across his back. Now, I've been eating right for three years, and I'm a little lighter than I used to be. But I still say it's a miracle that Junior was able to carry me through the Ozark brush, over fallen trees and under low branches, three hundred yards back to his car.

"Hang in there, Gary," he said several times.

I was busy praying and breathing, so I moaned a little in response.

But here's the amazing thing—Junior got us to the paramedics, they got us to the helicopter, and the helicopter got me to the hospital in time to save my life! So what started out to be a basic outdoor adventure turned into a death-defying race against time—a race that involved speeding emergency vehicles, blaring sirens, and emergency air travel in a medical helicopter.

GUY FACT

Each year more people are killed by donkeys than by plane crashes.

Which meant it was an outdoor adventure I'll never forget.

On a serious note, I believe prayer and Junior's heroic efforts saved my life. Doctors performed angioplasty on one of my arteries, which was completely blocked—the result of fifty-eight years of poor eating habits. My cardiologist and hospital nutritionist said that my change in eating habits over the past three years helped me avoid heart damage and aided me in a quick recovery. (I detailed those eating changes in my recent book *Food and Love*.)

I was sitting up in my hospital bed the next day, sending out e-mails about my adventure. Junior was the hero, and we'll always remain best friends because of that fateful day. I know I'd be in heaven had he not been there. And the bottom line was this: I had bagged a wild turkey in the process.

Many of us guys already have the relational tools necessary to relate to other men. We enjoy a good laugh, a shared experience, or an outdoor adventure, and we're friends for life. These types of guy relational tools are important. But if these are the only relational tools in our toolbox, we're limited—not just in our relationships with women, but with each other.

The truth is, our relationships with each other would be better if we'd learn a little more about the deeper relational tools, the ones we'll be taking a look at in the chapters ahead. That way we can share more than a laugh with a brother, father, son, or friend. We can share our hard times, our concerns, our questions. We can listen and be a support to the guys in our lives.

We can even tell them we love them.

If you're one of the guys who can already do this, good for you. Our guess is you've already got a grip on one or more of the relational tools. But it never hurts to rummage through the toolbox and see what tools you need to add to your collection. That's what we'll help you do in the chapters ahead.

Why Guys Have Trouble with Conversations

When it comes to relationships, one of the areas many guys fall short in is conversation.

Here's the problem: In the workplace most men use three primary tools to communicate—the fact-giving tool, the fact-finding tool, and the take-charge tool. While these are effective tools in that setting, they are not particularly helpful for building relationships.

We will look at the communication tools that can help make you a success when it comes to your relationships, but first let's take a look at the three communication tools found in most men's internal toolboxes and examine their weaknesses when it comes to personal relationships.

Let's start with the fact-giving tool, the one most of us guys seem to specialize in using when it comes to our relationships.

THE FACT-GIVING TOOL

The fact-giving tool is the ability to communicate the facts and nothing but the facts. This is a wonderful tool in the workplace when dialogue must be succinct and efficient. The problem—as we've suggested—is that too many men rely on this tool in their personal relationships. When we guys do that, then something like the following usually occurs.

It's been a long day on the job, and frankly you're beat. You park the car and head for the front door, where your wife greets you and says, "Hi, honey! How was your day?"

"Fine," you answer, and suddenly you can sense a scene like the one at the end of chapter 4 taking place right there in your own home.

After greeting your wife, you continue past the front door and into the kitchen, where you hope to find something cold to drink in the refrigerator. Your wife trails after you, still trying to engage you in some meaningful conversation. She hasn't seen you all day, and she's ready to talk.

GUY FACT

Loud talk can be ten times more distracting than the sound of a jackhammer.

"How was your meeting?" she asks, hoping for a lengthy, detailed answer.

Instead, you open the refrigerator, pull out a pop, and say, "Fine."

This "conversation" continues the same way through dinner. Your wife asks you pointed, open-ended questions, hoping to hear what you are thinking and how you are feeling, and the most you can relate to her is the basic facts of what happened at work that day. When the meal is over, instead of conversing with your wife you plop down in front of the television. You release a comfortable sigh, which an hour later will be replaced with snoring.

This is an adult version of the kind of communication used by the little boys in the study we cited in chapter 4. It's the communication of the facts and just the facts. Many guys limit their communication to functional communication—or fact giving. Like the little boys in that study, probably 60 percent of what you communicate in a given day is factual information. The other 40 percent is sounds: sighing, stretching, snoring. (We're not revealing any real secrets when we say guys are also known for other loud bodily noises.)

The Kind of Conversation Few Men Will Have

Let's examine the differences in the way many men and women communicate, using the following conversation as an example. As you read this, ask yourself if you can picture you and your buddies talking this way about anything.

Two women meet, and one notices a change in the other's hairstyle.

"Wow, Janice, did you get your hair cut?"

"Yes, I went to Classy Styles! It was amazing." She does a slight twirl and waves her fingers dramatically at her hair. "Don't you just love it?"

Studying each tendril of Janice's hair—the same way she might search for a lost contact lens—Janice's friend sucks in a deep breath. "It's absolutely to die for! It's so much better than when your *other* girl cuts it. And the style! I can't believe how thin it makes you look."

Janice wrinkles her nose. "You're sure it doesn't make my neck look too long?"

"Too long?" Her friend gasps. "Definitely not. You look like a model. Just the way it curls under and the extra shine. It'll make you feel better too. A new haircut always does." Janice takes another look. "What shampoo did she use?"

GUY FACT

The increase in the number of marriage and family therapists in the last decade is 50 percent.

"It was a salon mix, but she sold me a bottle anyway."

"You're kidding! It smells heavenly, and I can't believe the shine. You couldn't have a bad hair day with that shampoo."

"So you like the cut?"

"Definitely. It's you, completely."

"The stylist said it would help my shoulders look slimmer."

Janice gasps again. "She's right! I hadn't noticed it until now. No doubt about it." Janice's friend frowns. "I was just thinking that my shoulders look too broad lately. What's the phone number for the shop? I need something new too. A fresh look, a different attitude.

My hair's been looking mousy, and it's about time I made a change for the . . . "

It could go on that way for an hour and neither woman would get bored with the topic of Janice's new hairdo. With men, however, there would be a different version of this conversation: the fact-giving version.

THE FACT-GIVING VERSION

Take two men in the same situation as the one above. If one notices that his friend got a haircut, he might say something like, "You got your hair cut."

To which his friend would say something profound like, "Yep."

He might ask his friend where he had his hair cut and how much it cost—after all, those are facts a guy can use later on—but beyond that, the conversation about the haircut would be over.

Now, we know what you might be thinking right now: Of course these two guys didn't get into a lengthy, emotional conversation about a haircut. Most guys wouldn't even notice another guy's haircut unless it involved some sort of mistake.

Our point is that most men communicate using the fact-giving tool, and that includes the times they talk about things they may really care about. For example, let's say there are two guys who enjoy fishing. If one of them bought a brand-new rod and reel combination, he would simply state that fact to his buddy. No lengthy discussions about the emotional implications of a new rod and reel combination or whether this will or won't affect that guy's self-image. Just the facts.

"Hey, I got a new rod and reel."

"Great. Let's try it out sometime."

And that would be the end of it.

A Word Count Redux

Remember that daily word count we talked about earlier? The one dictated by the testosterone level in our brains? The one that for us men is less than half of a woman's daily word count? Many times we guys spend these words using the fact-giving tool. At work this might mean quite a bit of talking—details about a project, examples of how future work might get done, information to pass on to coworkers, etc.

Fact giving is very helpful in the work setting, but this type of communication tends to use up most of our words. And thus on the home front the already depleted fact-giving tool has a tendency to fall short.

The question-and-answer session detailed in the last chapter is proof enough.

Think back to that dialogue and see if it doesn't come awfully close to what you're used to. It might even make you laugh out loud. It did for our wives. Why? Because even though we're aware of our word deficiencies, we still have a tendency to run low on dialogue once we get home at night.

After a question-and-answer session like that one, the woman is thinking, *If he really loved me, he'd talk to me.*

But come on, guys. Is that what we're thinking? Are we thinking we're angry at our wife, that we don't like her, that she isn't important, or even that we don't care what she has to say that night? Of course not!

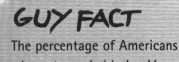

GUY FACT
The percentage of Americans who get married in Las Vegas is 4 percent.

More often than not, we are thinking of factual things, like how good it is to be home, how we wish she'd give us a hug, how long it is until dinner, and how we can finally relax now that the day is over. In truth, when our wives ask us about our day, most of us are genuinely glad she's interested.

In chapter 4 we included one of those question-and-answer sessions between a man and his wife, where she asked the questions and he gave his one-word answers. We know that conversation sounded extreme, but our research has shown us that this type of conversation is common. Too common.

If a conversation like that has ever taken place in your home, the woman you love may speak fourteen times as many words as you. And in a few hours she'll have reached her word count, all right. But she'll be so frustrated with trying to engage you in conversation that she'll want to go to bed early and sleep with her back to you, balanced on the edge of the mattress.

TOOL TIP

In order for most of us guys to be better communicators, we need to add to our daily word count by adding to our relational toolbox.

Over the past few years we've done surveys on this subject at dozens of our seminars and conferences. We ask women about the internal tools in the toolboxes of the men they love. Then we ask how those tools work in a relationship. Their responses are striking. Sort of like a sledgehammer on a thumbtack.

Here are some of the things women said about the fact-giving tool as men use it in their relationships:

✗ "He doesn't want to share his heart with me."
✗ "He tells me things that sound like a news report rather than loving thoughts."
✗ "I feel like his boss, like he's checking in with me rather than sharing with me."
✗ "He doesn't have time for me."
✗ "He's become shallow and uninteresting, given only to factual answers."

Are you gaining some understanding here, something that could help you understand the woman you love? If you're a fact giver, we certainly hope so. We want you to understand that your wife isn't mad at you, doesn't hate you, and isn't bored with your company. She's simply hurt because you're using your fact-giving tool in the wrong situation. To remedy that, you will need to reach for some entirely different tools. We'll discuss that a bit later.

For now, though, let's take an in-depth look at the usual companion to the fact-giving tool—the fact-finding tool.

THE FACT-FINDING TOOL

If you are like a lot of guys, when the conversation between you and a loved one gets to the point where the woman sighs and says, "Honey, I want to talk . . . ," usually the first thing out of your mouth will be, "About what?"

That's the fact-finding tool in action.

In the words of Joe Friday in the movie *Dragnet,* we guys want "the facts, ma'am, nothing but the facts." And as soon as the woman runs out of facts, we become bored and uninterested.

For instance, if a teenage daughter wants to talk about her day, most of us guys will listen through the part about getting an A on the science test and having an English essay on South America due next week. But when she veers into a dissertation about her friend Mindy and how Mindy thinks it's okay to have lots of friends but Cassie doesn't like Mindy and what will that mean for the coming school dance—well, most of us guys will tune out. Here are some hurtful things we guys who use our fact-finding tools are likely to say if a woman launches into a lengthy discussion about something that doesn't involve facts:

✗ "What's the point?"
✗ "Is this going somewhere?"
✗ "How long is this conversation going to take?"
✗ "What are you trying to say?"
✗ "We're moving into relationship stuff here, aren't we?"

Obviously, these questions don't help our relationships. In fact, they can be quite damaging. This is why, when it comes to talking to their loved ones, many guys need to make use of internal tools other than their fact-finding tools.

Now let's take a look at the fact-finding tool in action.

The Remote Control and the Fact-Finding Tool

This will not be a news flash, but most men are notorious TV remote control addicts. Some of us can watch upwards of five or six programs at once by flipping channels with the remote and still have a general sense of what's happening in every one of them. Or as comedian Jerry Seinfeld said, "Men don't want to know what's on television. They want to know what *else* is on television." On the other hand, women can feel practically nauseous having so many channels and programs coming into the room at one time. This is an example of the fact-finding tool in action.

Let's say, for instance, that a couple sits down to watch television. The first program they check out is an old Western movie. Right away they focus on different things. After one minute here's the scenario:

WHAT A WOMAN MIGHT BE THINKING	WHAT A MAN MIGHT BE THINKING
Who is that woman, anyway?	If I turn the channel now, I can get back to this in five minutes and find out if the woman lived.
Is she someone's girlfriend or wife?	I think *Sports Center* is about to start.
Does she have children?	I wonder what the weather was like in Florida today?
Why does the robber want her?	Is this the night the *Crocodile Hunter* reruns air on Animal Planet?
Is he in love with her?	Wasn't there a baseball game on one of the cable channels?

Can you see the problem here?

Most women will be caught up in emotional aspects of the program while we men are, for the most part, content with knowing the facts. And in that light, most television programs contain too much emotional filler for our tastes. Only by flipping channels will we obtain the maximum amount of fact-finding in a given hour of TV viewing.

In a nutshell, most women want relational-type programs,

whether it's *Oprah* or a Hallmark movie of the week. Most men, however, are looking for information—who won the game, who scored the goal, who rescued the woman in the Western. Some women who don't particularly like sports say they become interested in a televised game if they can feel connected to a player's life. Once they feel emotionally bonded to a player, they enjoy the game.

The differences in the television-viewing habits of men and women are just one example of the man's fact-finding tool at work. But there are others, and some of them can do great damage to relationships. According to our surveys, here are some examples of what women think of men who overuse their fact-finding tool within their relationships:

✗ "He doesn't care about my feelings, just the facts."
✗ "He does not hear my heart but jumps to conclusions."
✗ "He interrupts me when I have something deep to say."
✗ "He is narrow-minded and dogmatic, interested only in solving problems."
✗ "As far as he's concerned, the sooner the conversation is over, the better."

Ouch! Do some of these comments ring true of you? If so, there's hope.

Most of us guys are simply not very interested in conversation that's not about facts. And this is painful for most women. It's one of the areas where problems can spring up in our relationships. It's also not very healthy for us men. It is always better for our mental and physical health if we can express our feelings. Help in doing that is on the way. If you don't already have the right tools to express your feelings, we will show you several that will help you communicate better.

First, though, let's look more closely at the third internal tool that tends to affect how we communicate.

TAKE-CHARGE TOOL

The take-charge tool is the ability to assess a situation and take control of it. As we've mentioned, this is a wonderful tool in the workplace. But most of the time this is the wrong tool for relationships. Take a look at how a man's use of the take-charge tool nearly ruined an afternoon at the mall.

TOOL TIP

The fact-giving, fact-finding, and take-charge tools work great in the workplace but not as well in personal relationships.

Women see a shopping trip as a relaxing couple of hours to chat and catch up on the week's news. This might mean browsing through one shop after another to see what fashions are in style. Men, on the other hand, generally see the outing as a time to take charge and conquer. In other words, get in there, find what you want, buy it, and go home.

Here is an example.

"I'm going shopping," a woman tells her husband. "Wanna come?"

The man thinks about that for a moment. "Shopping for what?"

"I need a new purse."

"Your old purse is broken?" He blinks, certain she had used the purse the night before and also certain that it was in fine working condition. For a purse, that is.

"No, silly. It's not broken. It's just not . . . " she hesitates, searching for the right word. "It's not 'me' anymore. I need a new one."

"You *want* a new one, you mean."

"Okay." She laughs and reaches for her husband's hand. "Wanna come with me?" She's thinking, *This will be wonderful. Just the two of us, strolling through the mall, spending time alone together, walking hand in hand. We'll laugh and catch up on things at work and maybe stop for coffee before we go home.*

But he's thinking, *We'll get the new purse and be home in time to watch the playoffs.* Already he has the take-charge tool out of his internal toolbox.

"Okay," he says. "Let's go."

Fifteen minutes later they arrive at the mall, and he finds a front-row parking spot—which is the first step toward conquering the purse. Walking toward the mall entrance, the woman takes the man's hand.

"This'll be fun." She smiles.

He nods, distracted, and leads her inside, where he says, "Where's the purse store?"

"Purse store?" She utters a short laugh. "There are no purse stores, exactly." She gestures toward the length of the mall. "Purses are sold at almost every store in the mall."

"Fine." He points at the nearest store. "Let's get one."

She looks hard at him as though he's speaking a foreign language. "We don't have to get the first purse we see, do we?"

And the man is thinking, *Did I miss something? I thought she needed a purse.* "What else do you need?" he asks.

His words are like thumbtacks poking holes in her heart. He's already casting a shadow of frustration on the date she'd imagined at the mall. "Well," she says, "I wanted to look around. I need a gift for a baby shower next week and then there's your mother's birthday and . . ."

GUY FACT

The average number of stores a couple will visit before they decide on an engagement ring is 4.6.

"You didn't say anything about that," he says. He is doing his best to keep an even tone, but at this point he can sense he's losing the battle. He draws a steadying breath. "You said we were coming for a purse. You needed a new purse."

He has the take-charge tool in full use now.

If the tears aren't already in her eyes by now, they're definitely forming. "Fine. Let's go," she says.

They start walking, only this time her arms are crossed, her steps quick and irritated. In very little time they arrive at a department store with a section of purses the size of a bookstore. Hundreds of purses in dozens of different textures, sizes, and colors crowd the section. He is thinking, *We've found it! The purse is as good as purchased!*

And she's thinking, *Fine, if he doesn't want to look around, at least I can take my time picking out a new purse.*

They walk inside, and he watches her slowly make the round along the inside perimeter of the purse display. Irritated that she isn't finding anything, he comes alongside her. "Honey, what are you looking for?"

"Well, something comfortable . . . " She's thinking he's being downright awful. If he's in that kind of hurry to be done with their date together, then how much does he really enjoy being with her, anyway? If he really loved her, she's thinking, he'd want to walk slowly through the mall, holding hands and talking about whatever comes to mind.

Meanwhile, he's wondering what would she do without him. If it weren't for his role in this mission, she might never find a purse. "Okay, honey," he says, "let's narrow it down . . . comfortable, meaning what exactly?"

The search turns up nothing. Not a single one of the purses in the store is "comfortable" to his wife. But the man is not daunted. He's gone hunting before and knows that it often takes more than one effort to bag the prize catch. The same is probably true with a new purse. Besides, as long as they find something in the next forty minutes, he'll still make it home in time for the game.

Three stores later, it's become a contest, a challenge to find the ultimate prize—the perfect purse. The exact purse that will suit his wife's taste, wherever that purse may be. He's thinking, *Whether the game starts without me or not, we will find that purse.* That's his competitive-drive tool at work. (We'll talk about that in more detail in the next chapter.) Anything short of driving home with the right purse would leave him with the same size pit in his stomach he got as a high school boy when his team missed the state basketball playoffs by a single basket.

To come this close, to be surrounded by purses and miss the one

> **GUY FACT**
>
> The number of marriages per week in Las Vegas is 1,700.

that his wife so deeply needs and desires is not even conceivable. So he urges her on to the next and last department store in the mall.

There it finally happens. The woman finds a smallish leather purse, tries it on, and smiles. "Well . . . it's comfortable."

The man's heart races. "It looks comfortable," he agrees. "Let's buy it."

Her eyes meet his and he can see she's surprised. "We can't just buy it like that. Let me look at it for a minute."

The man stares at the purse. To him it looks like a purse. In fact, it looks a lot like the old purse back at home. "What are we looking for?" he asks.

She slips it over her shoulder. "Does it make me look fat?"

The man starts to say it's just a purse and how can a purse make a person look fat, but then he realizes that the game isn't played that way. In order to conquer the situation, he must give the proper answer. "No, not at all, dear," he assures her. "The purse makes you look very comfortable."

GUY FACT

The estimated number of marriage and family therapists in the U.S. is 50,000.

"Comfortable?" There is a cry in her voice. "I don't want to *look* comfortable. I want to *feel* comfortable."

Holding off his panic, the man swallows hard. "I mean, it makes you look thin, dear. Very thin."

"You think so?"

"Definitely."

And with that—after more than an hour of searching—she decides it's the right purse for her. She's thinking, *I'm glad it took awhile longer. This has been nice after all, spending extra time together and having him help me find the purse I want. How sweet is that, anyway?*

His thoughts are focused on the yellow tag attached to the purse. *It's on sale!* That's like hitting a prize buck with a towering rack of horns. It's like catching the biggest fish of the day in the last five minutes before turning in.

Walking out of the mall minutes later, this man gladly offers to carry the bag. Why? Because he is feeling victorious. His heart is beating hard with thoughts of, W*e did it! We hunted down our trophy purse!*

This shopping expedition is a perfect illustration of the take-charge tool in action. There was a mission: finding a purse. And with some not-so-gentle prodding and "encouragement," he was able to get his wife to finally buy the purse she wanted. But at the same time, his take-charge, competitive attitude created conflict between his wife and him.

That is what happens when a man reaches into his internal toolbox and pulls out the take-charge tool in his relationships.

The Take-Charge Tool in the Workplace

What does the take-charge tool look like in the work setting? Research done by social psychologists Nancy Henley and Cheris Kramarae shows men are more likely to dominate women socially by interrupting a conversation.[1]

In general, research shows the take-charge tool at work this way:

✗ Language patterns between men and women show a man's conversation to be associated with dominance, a woman's with powerlessness and submissiveness.
✗ Some women will admit that they defer to men in conversation because they fear seeming aggressive and "unfeminine."
✗ Women are generally more uncomfortable than men when it comes to speaking in public situations.
✗ Men interrupt women more often than the reverse.

Now let's imagine what this same dynamic looks like in our personal relationships with the women in our lives.

The Shortcomings of the Take-Charge Tool

We put together a series of detailed surveys and gave them to thousands of women in the past few years. One of the questions we asked was, What does it look like for a man to use his take-charge tool in a relationship? Here are some of the responses we received:

✗ "He forgets that we're a team."

✗ "He talks over me, ignores my opinions and comments, doesn't seek my advice."

✗ "He's often overbearing and domineering, thinking he knows best and not needing any input from me."

✗ "He's often controlling and doesn't take my needs into account."

✗ "I feel that he always needs to be the captain and that every decision is his."

So there you have it. Fact-giving, fact-finding, and take-charge tools—the very ones that serve us so well in the business world—don't work nearly as well when it comes to our personal relationships, particularly with women.

But isn't this true with all tools? They have specific purposes, but when used for the wrong job, they can fall short—sometimes disastrously so.

That was certainly the case for a guy named Gavin.

THE WRONG TOOL FOR THE JOB

It was Saturday, and Gavin's wife was headed out to the mall for some major back-to-school shopping. She was taking both of their children, so Gavin figured it would be a wonderful afternoon to catch a ball game on TV and take a nap. Possibly even at the same time.

Gavin's wife had other ideas.

"Dear, if you could get to the basement today, I'd really appreciate it."

Gavin knew his wife well enough to know that she really meant, "You better not spend the day sitting in your recliner."

Silence filled the room while Gavin's wife waited expectantly. Then with a sad and heavy sigh, Gavin nodded. "Yes, dear."

And with that, his wife and children left the house in search of school clothes.

For a long while after, Gavin sat in his recliner and thought about the task ahead.

The family's basement had slipped past the point of unkempt and plodded full-bore into the area of unsafe. Gavin's mother had died a year earlier, and Gavin's basement had become the resting place for dozens of her boxes. Boxes filled with newspapers, tax records, bank statements, and hundreds of old books.

In the process, what once was a play area for the kids was now little more than a glorified storage space. It took about three weeks before the local spiders discovered the fact. Now, Gavin lived in Missouri not far from the Smalley Relationship Center. We have it fairly good here in the Ozarks—not many tornadoes, limited amounts of snowfall, a few days of ice each year.

But we do have this little spider called the brown recluse. And once it's made its way into a person's house and started building little funnel webs throughout storage boxes, some people find it easier to simply move.

Gavin considered that as he sat in his recliner that afternoon. But then his problem-solving tool kicked in. He could don a long-sleeve shirt, jeans, and a pair of protective gloves and make his way meticulously around the basement, clearing one web after another. Or . . .

A wonderful idea came to Gavin.

And in that moment he firmly took hold of his problem-solving tool.

He didn't have to spend a perfectly wonderful Saturday afternoon cleaning cobwebs in the basement. No, sir. Not when he had the tool to do the job more quickly. A surge of adrenaline coursed through his veins, and he fairly leapt up from his chair and headed toward the garage.

Gavin was a toolhound. If you aren't a toolhound, you certainly know one. A toolhound is someone who simply has to have the newest, biggest, best tool, even if he might never use it in his lifetime. Because of that, when Sears advertised a sale on blowtorches the month before, Gavin about went crazy until he finally drove his truck down to Sears and bought one for himself.

"Why in the world do you need a blowtorch?" his wife asked him.

"They're on sale," Gavin said, his mouth dropping a bit in aston-ishment. "They've *never* been on sale."

His wife blinked. "But you don't need a blowtorch."

"I might someday," Gavin countered. "Besides they're better than they used to be, more efficient. There are lots of jobs that require a blowtorch."

"Hanging a picture? Changing out the faucet in the bathroom?" Gavin's wife used these examples because those were the types of jobs she was always hoping Gavin might do with his tools.

But Gavin had far grander ideas.

"Of course not." He gave a short laugh. "A blowtorch is something I might need to fix the car one day . . . something that could save us thousands of dollars."

Gavin's wife looked doubtful, but she didn't volley a counter-attack. She knew better because she—more than anyone else—under-stood that Gavin was a toolhound. Better just to let him get the tool and stash it away until the moment when—or if—he might actually need it for something.

And that day, with his family out shopping, Gavin knew that the blowtorch was just the tool he needed to clear those pesky cobwebs. He grabbed it from its shelf, took it from the box, and made sure it was in working order. Then he trotted back into the house, down the stairs, and into the basement.

The place was crawling with cobwebs.

Gavin figured the fix would go something like this: Since cobwebs are made of fine, delicate fibers, he would fire up the blowtorch in the direction of the webs and . . . *poof!* In an instant an entire section of the room would undergo cobweb evaporation. A few quick bursts from the blowtorch and he could call it a day, flop back in his chair, and set about his original plans for the afternoon.

It didn't quite work out that way.

Gavin positioned himself in the center of the basement and aimed the blowtorch toward the southeast corner.

"Here goes . . . " he said to himself.

Then he pulled the trigger. *Whoooosh!*

What happened next was something he had to explain several times as the day unfolded. First to the fire department, then to his wife and kids. As it turned out, the blowtorch was somewhat stronger than Gavin expected. One pull on the trigger and the torch shot a stream of flames that pretty much consumed not only the cobwebs but both the south and east walls of the basement.

GUY FACT

According to *The Guinness Book of Records,* the longest marriage lasted eighty-six years; the couple was Sir Temulji Bhicaji Nariman and Lady Nariman, who were wed when they were five years old.

Instantly the room burst into flames, fueled by his mother's many boxes and who knows how many brown recluse spiders. Gavin escaped with his blowtorch and his life and made it upstairs to call 911. By the time the fire department arrived, the basement and the main floor were pretty much a loss.

"I guess it was the wrong tool for the job," Gavin said later.

The same is true when we guys try to use the fact-finding, fact-giving, and take-charge tools when trying to communicate with someone we love. Those are just the wrong tools for the job.

In the next chapter we'll take a look at why our other internal tools make us difficult to live with. Now remember, these tools are important—even crucial—when it comes to protecting and providing. But they can be as destructive as a blowtorch when it comes to sharing a meal or an afternoon—or especially a house—with the women we love.

Why Guys
Have Trouble Bonding

One of the most popular books about the differences between men and women is *Men Are from Mars, Women Are from Venus* by John Gray. This book goes into detail about why men and women struggle so much in relating to one another.

And we do struggle.

We Smalley guys believe men struggle in their relationships because they try to use the wrong internal tools for the job. In this chapter we'd like to look at three more internal tools God has equipped us with. We want to look at their strengths as they relate to our provider-protector roles and their weaknesses when it comes to relating to those we love the most.

Let's start by looking at the tool that helps us men when it's time to get things done.

WHAT THE TASK-ORIENTED TOOL LOOKS LIKE
God has wired us guys to take care of business, to complete the tasks assigned to us. As we said earlier, men have been using that internal tool—the task-oriented tool—since the beginning of time.

We believe that we guys are often more task oriented and less emotional or relational simply because we have been conditioned to be that way. We once counseled a guy who was a perfect example of this. Here's his story.

Mark was extremely task oriented. He was a fantastic doer. When he was given a list of tasks, he prided himself on finishing them first and best. But he had almost no ability to relate to his wife and children on an emotional level.

The problem?

Mark grew up in a home where the expression of feelings was forbidden. His father barked commands at him, but never—not once that Mark could remember—did his father demonstrate his love. He never put an arm around Mark's shoulders and drew him close, never kissed him on the forehead, never patted him on the back. And Mark's dad never said the words every boy needs so desperately to hear: "I love you, Son."

GUY FACT

According to experts, 30 percent of all marriages occur because of friendship.

Instead, his father pushed Mark to accomplish whatever task he set before him. His father instilled in him the attitude that it had to be done the best it could be, and anything less than that was failure. When Mark did something well, that was what was expected. But when he failed or when he responded to a situation in a way his father didn't like, he was in trouble.

As an adult, Mark never thought much about how emotionally closed off his father was until one dark winter day when a policeman knocked at his door. The news was something every parent dreads. Mark's thirteen-year-old son had been riding his bike and was hit by a drunk driver. He died at the scene.

Mark was angry and hurt, but he was unable to cry then—or days later at his son's graveside service.

"I saw my wife shed tears of sorrow, and I watched the hurt expressed by many of our friends and family members," he told us. "But as much as I wanted to, I couldn't release my grief with tears. I just couldn't feel it. I bottled up the pain inside and pulled back into a shell."

Then, a few weeks after the funeral, God did something very special to open Mark's eyes to what had happened in his heart.

Mark told us he was out in his workshop working on a project, trying to take his mind off what had happened. Again, this was Mark's task-oriented tool at work. Mark thought he could deal with his buried emotional pain by getting something accomplished, by finishing a task.

He was sanding a piece of fairly rough pine when his finger slid along the edge of the board. Just then a long, needle-sharp splinter was shoved almost an inch into his thumb. The pain was excruciating, and as he pulled the splinter from his thumb, it began bleeding profusely.

GUY FACT

More than 110,000 marriage licenses are issued in Las Vegas each year.

Mark stood there in the workshop—tears in his eyes, his thumb throbbing—and suddenly he was ten years old again. A picture began to form in his mind of a day on a lake. He and his father were fishing, and his father was yelling at him. Mark waited as the memory took shape fully, and then he remembered why his father had been angry.

In his childlike hurry, Mark had fallen and hooked his thumb on a long, barbed fishhook. His father made him pull the fishhook out. Then the angry man began shouting at Mark for crying and having tears in his eyes. Next he beat him in a way Mark remembers to this day.

"Men do not cry," his father yelled as the beating continued.

The memory faded.

At that moment—there in the workshop behind his home, just weeks after his own son's death—Mark suddenly realized he had been living under that cloud ever since: *Men aren't allowed to feel.*

"When my son died, it was like a metal sword pierced my heart," Mark told us. "But I couldn't show any emotion because I had come to believe that men don't cry or show their feelings."

Even if their feelings have to be beaten out of them.

Mark knew that he couldn't move another inch without removing the metal sword from his heart. Yes, it would bleed, but it would never heal any other way. So then and there, overwhelmed by the picture of his past and the emotion that had been dammed up in his heart for weeks, he began to shake.

The metal sword was suddenly gone, and tears—real tears—began to flow from his eyes. An accomplished task would not rid his heart of the ocean of pain that had built up there.

For what felt like hours, Mark stood in his workshop, sobbing, weeping for the boy he'd lost. It was the first time he could remember crying.

But thankfully it hasn't been the last.

He told us recently, "I know now that Jesus doesn't mind my tears, and he feels my pain. That day in the workshop, it was as if he said to me, 'Your busy tasks will not help you deal with emotional pain. I know all about your splinters. I felt them when I was on the cross. But I love you enough to let you cry and to hug away your hurt.' "

A man who can cry is a man who has learned some secrets about the basic relational tools. But sadly, for many of us it takes something tragic or life changing before we understand this truth.

Here are a few ways you can tell if you have trouble expressing your feelings:

✗ You're unable or unwilling to discuss your feelings.
✗ You're unable or unwilling to cry.
✗ You're determined to make all situations into a joke.
✗ You're determined to lighten the mood or change the topic when emotional issues are discussed.
✗ You tend to leave the room or change the subject when emotional issues come up.

You may be an extremely task-oriented guy who doesn't have enough capacity to feel in your relationships. That may have started when you were a boy. As a young person you might have gone through something traumatic with your father or mother or cousins or uncles. You may have been told "Don't cry unless you're hurt," "Tough it out," "Boys don't cry," or "Only sissies get hurt feelings." The underlying message is this: "It's a sign of weakness to let people see your feelings."

TOOL TIP

A man who can cry is a man who has learned some secrets about the basic relational tools.

When a young male brain is saturated in testosterone, it doesn't take much, even from well-meaning family members, for a boy to get the message that emotions and feelings are for girls and that the main job of real men is to do their tasks and do them well.

The Weaknesses of the Task-Oriented Tool

If you are the kind of guy who regularly reaches into his internal toolbox for his task-oriented tool, then you are more than likely bottled up inside, unable to express your feelings. Guys like you tend to have a determined personality and a conquering nature. You are more driven by accomplishments than by relationships.

In contrast, most women tend to be less task oriented and more people oriented. They tend to be more aware of others' feelings, and they also tend to build their days around the emotional needs of those they love. The tasks before them will always take a backseat to the emotions of their loved ones.

Okay, let's take a look at how women view men who rely too much on the task-oriented tool. We interviewed hundreds of women at our seminars to get their input. While almost all the women we interviewed appreciated how this tool worked to protect and provide for them, they also said it was often destructive when it came to their relationships. Here are some of the specific things the women had to say about the task-oriented tool:

✗ "He's always pushing to accomplish something and move to the next achievement."
✗ "His achievements or accomplishments are more important than his relationship with me and our family."
✗ "He's strong and controlling, wanting everything to be perfect."
✗ "It feels like I am a conquest and not a partner. With sex, he would rather get down to business than be involved in foreplay."
✗ "It seems that what he does is more important than who we are together."

Do you see yourself in these comments? If so, there is hope for you. Later we'll talk about the tools you can acquire that will help you relate with your loved ones on a more emotional level.

For now, however, let's take a look at the next internal tool most of us guys have in our toolboxes: the problem-solving tool.

GUYS AND THE PROBLEM-SOLVING TOOL

Men and women approach problems with similar goals but different considerations. While men and women can solve problems equally well, their approach and their process are often quite different. For most women, sharing and discussing a problem presents an opportunity to explore, deepen, or strengthen relationships. Women are usually more concerned about *how* problems are solved than *if* they are solved. The process of solving a problem can strengthen or weaken a relationship.

Most men are less concerned about relationships when solving a problem. For most men, solving a problem presents an opportunity to demonstrate their competence, their strength of resolve, and their commitment to a relationship. How the problem is solved is not nearly as important as solving it effectively and in the best possible manner. Men have a tendency to dominate and to assume authority in a problem-solving process. They are not often focused on the quality of relationships while solving problems.

Some of the more important differences can be illustrated by observing groups of teenage boys and groups of teenage girls attempting to find their way out of a maze. Boys generally establish a hierarchy, choosing a leader who emerges on his own or through demonstrations of ability and power. Boys explore the maze using scouts while remaining in distant proximity to each other. Groups of girls tend to explore the maze together as a group without establishing a clear or dominant leader. Relationships tend to be coequal. Girls tend to discuss the problem and apply "collective intelligence" to the task of discovering a way out.[1]

What is your style of solving problems? Are you the kind of guy who excels at looking at a problem or a puzzle and quickly and efficiently coming up with a solution? Can you look at a malfunction in your car or around the house and see in moments what needs to be done? If so, you are probably adept at using the problem-solving tool.

We guys tend to be good at problem solving. It's part of who we are, part of how God designed us. Here is a good example of a man who used the problem-solving tool with great skill.

Bob fit very nicely into the generalizations we've been talking about. He liked factual statements and situations, and at first he resisted helping his wife, Betty, with housework.

"I didn't know what to do," he explained to us.

But in an effort to truly honor his wife, Bob chose to become a new man. The problem was, he did it by using his problem-solving tool. Now, the use of this tool can be a good thing. But in this case, mere problem solving was too simple for the tasks his wife expected him to do. This became particularly evident once when Betty asked him to clean the downstairs bathroom.

"Sure, honey," Bob told her. He grabbed his problem-solving tool and headed to the bathroom, armed with a bucket, sponges, sprays, and powders.

What he saw came as a complete surprise: The bathroom was already clean. Bob looked around to make sure he was right. There was no dirt in the sink, none in the toilet, and none on the floors. He shook his head in confusion and tucked his problem-solving tool back in his toolbox. If the bathroom was already clean, then the problem was solved.

GUY FACT

According to studies conducted at Northwestern University, women tend to take longer than men to make a decision but are more likely to stick to it.

He returned the cleaning supplies to the laundry room and then reported to Betty.

"It's clean," he said. Then he smiled for good measure.

"What?" Betty's eyebrows knitted into two tense, crooked lines. "That's impossible."

She led the way as the two of them returned to the bathroom. Betty walked through the door, did a single glance about the room, and put her hands on her hips. "What do you mean, 'It's clean'?" She grimaced at the sink. "It's filthy."

Bob followed Betty's gaze and squinted. For the life of him he couldn't see any dirt. From Betty's tone of voice, he'd have expected to see whole colonies of mold and bacteria with germs the size of house pets.

"It looks clean to me." Bob shrugged.

At that, Betty's expression fell. You see, on some level Betty thought that cleaning the bathroom would be—at least partially—an emotional experience. She wanted Bob to appreciate the level of cleaning she did on a regular basis. Then she wanted him to duplicate that type of cleaning. But Bob was seeing the situation only as a problem to be solved, and since the bathroom looked clean, there was no longer a problem.

Betty rolled her eyes and said, "If you cared about me, Bob, you'd make an effort."

Make an effort? Bob was baffled. "It doesn't need cleaning. How can that mean I don't care about you?"

The disagreement became an argument that repeated itself every weekend for a month.

Since then, Bob has learned to use a few of the relational tools in addition to his problem-solving one. Now he simply attacks the room as if it *did* have germs the size of house pets, and even though he sees no difference in the before and after pictures, Betty is thrilled. This way Bob is still able to use his problem-solving tool, but he's also learned to honor Betty and to compromise on what exactly defines clean in their household.

What the Problem-Solving Tool Can and Can't Do

So why can't we guys build a common bond with the ones we love? Because we tend to be busy solving problems. We want to jump in and identify and tackle our problems—as well as our loved one's problems. We want to look for a solution and apply it without wavering—and more often than not, without emotion or feeling.

Women, on the other hand, tend to keep themselves busy probing the emotions that surround problems and issues. They tend to look for emotional issues behind a problem and can be swayed toward one of several solutions, depending on the emotional aspect of a problem. To some of us men this can look out of balance and complicated.

Bob merely wanted to find the shortest way to a clean bathroom. Betty took that as a lack of effort and as a personal slight to who she was as a person.

It's time to see what the women have to say about this issue. Again, we took these answers from the surveys we've taken at our conferences over the past few years. These are some of the things women say about what happens when a man relies on his problem-solving tool:

✗ "Instead of just listening, he tries to fix my problems."
✗ "He wants to see problems gone, not resolved and fully worked through."
✗ "He can be a control freak."
✗ "He takes responsibility for my problems and doesn't allow me time to think about a solution."
✗ "He thinks he has all the answers."

There's no question that the problem-solving tool is great when it comes to taking care of problems around the office or around the house. But it lacks something when it comes to relating with our loved ones. If you tend to be so task oriented that you sometimes treat the ones you love more as problems to be solved than people, don't despair—there is hope for you. But first let's take a look at the last tool most of us guys tend to have in our internal toolboxes: the competitive-drive tool.

THE COMPETITIVE-DRIVE TOOL (A.K.A. A GUY'S WILL TO WIN)

Nearly every guy we've met comes equipped with what we call the competitive-drive tool. We use that particular internal tool in many arenas: work, sporting activities, and outdoor recreation (just listen to two guys on a fishing trip argue about whose fish was bigger, and you'll see what we mean). Let's face it, guys: We love to win, and most of us will do whatever it takes to accomplish that goal.

We once counseled a pastor who had a problem controlling his competitive-drive tool. People were leaving this pastor's church because of his out-of-balance desire to win.

The congregation was small—three hundred—and many of the people enjoyed getting together for church picnics and recreational nights. The problem was that no matter what the activity, the pastor had to be better than the other men. If they played basketball, he delivered as many cheap shots as he needed to get the rebound or basket. If they played touch football, he'd shamelessly beat out a ten-year-old for the ball and run it into the end zone. If they had a watermelon-eating contest, he'd rather get sick than let someone else walk away with the trophy. Even if they hiked a local mountain trail—we're talking about a leisurely recreational hike, not a race—this pastor would forgo conversation and walking with the group to press his way twenty yards ahead of everyone else to the end point of the hike. That way he could feel as if he had somehow "won" the hike.

The relationships with the people in this pastor's congregation weren't the only ones his overly competitive nature was hurting. "What hurts is that his attitude is carrying over into our relationship," the pastor's wife told us. "I know for sure that four families have left because the men feel bugged by my husband's attitude. And I'm hoping I won't be next."

After weeks of discussion with this young pastor, we determined that the only way to fix the problem was for him to remove himself from the church's activities and instead take on a leadership role—making the rounds at social events and overseeing the activities as they unfolded.

TOOL TIP

*When it comes to work and competitive events,
use your competitive-drive tool sparingly, keeping in mind
that you are competing with real people.*

In the process, he took up hunting and club basketball as a way of venting his competitive nature outside the realm of the church.

This story demonstrates what we've observed over and over in our counseling and seminars: The competitive-drive tool is fantastic for business and intense sporting events, but when it comes to relating with people, it's best left in the toolbox.

Gary discovered that while he was performing one of the basic duties of a husband and father: driving. We'll let him tell the story.

Gary, the Road Warrior

My wife and I discovered my own overzealous desire to win when we drove on vacations. We still laugh about the times we prepared to take off and I'd strategize about traveling 500 miles a day. I wanted to make time and reach a certain goal each day. My wife, Norma, had other plans—plans to see the sights and the cute little shops along the way.

Even now when I have a destination in mind, I want to win. The solution is getting to that destination as quickly as possible. I want to get in the car, take off, and get to my destination—without distractions.

On trips we took when our children were younger, I hated to pull over for any reason—even when my wife or kids needed to use the rest room. It was also tough for me to pull off the freeway into one of those fast-food restaurants for lunch. Instead, I wanted us to pack lunches so we could keep hauling. If we had to stop for gas, I would allow my family to hurry and use the rest room. But the whole time, I'd watch the freeway, see cars I'd passed miles ago fly by, and mutter something about why couldn't my family hurry up.

It's only been in recent years that I realized something: It doesn't make me the winner to get there fast. In fact, I've learned that leisure time with my loved ones is not the time for me to use the competitive-drive tool. These days I do my best to keep that tool tucked safely away when we vacation. Using that tool during our driving trips only drove a wedge between Norma and me and made me seem like a tyrant.

And that's hard for anyone to live with.

The Lesson to Learn: A Relationship Is Not about Competition
A guy who has an extremely competitive attitude may be willing to emotionally or physically crush people who stand between him and his victory, trophy, or goal. It doesn't matter what activity he's involved in, this kind of guy will have a single-minded, focused determination to win. That can harm his relationships with his wife, children, extended family members, coworkers, and friends. In the extreme, this mind-set causes feuds, fights, abuse, crime, wars, even murders.

Many women have strong competitive drives. But our research shows that even a competitive woman still tends to value the experience and the relationships above the win. Women tend to be careful, using their strength with control. Even when they exert their power, they do it with others in mind.

This is not the case with many guys. We tend to exert our power, using brute force if necessary. We can "play rough" and have a win-or-else mentality. We men tend to value the competition itself over the relationships that can form as a result.

Let's see what women think of how men wield this particular internal tool in their relationships. Again, we asked the women in our seminars what it looks like when a man uses his competitive-drive tool in a relationship. These were some of their answers:

✗ "He tries to 'fix' me and convince me his way is the right way."
✗ "A challenge conjures up in him the need to compete, to try to win at all costs."
✗ "He seems to enjoy arguing and disagreeing with me."
✗ "He's always looking to be right and better than I am."
✗ "He likes to antagonize me and be confrontational."

Sound familiar? Obviously the competitive-drive tool lacks something—and that's a big understatement—when it comes to our relationships with the people we love. We guys need to remember that—and then leave it in the toolbox.

If in reading this chapter you see yourself using these internal tools in your relationships and if you've seen that these tools have fallen short, take heart. Keep reading, and you'll have a chance to acquire the tools you'll need to live and love and even work together with the people you care about.

Now let's move on and discuss the importance of using the right tool at the right time to make our relationships all they can be.

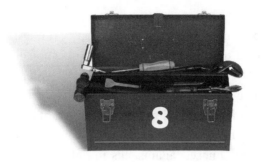

Reaching for the Right Tools

We've taken a good look at the tools most men already have, the internal tools that make us successful as providers and protectors. Now let's take a look at the tools we might need to add to our internal toolbox.

You may already have some of the relational tools we'll talk about. Or you may already have all but one of the relational tools we'll talk about in this chapter; but that one tool you add might take your relationships from mediocre to amazing.

For now, though, the bottom line is that you know there is something you need. And that reminds us of a story about John, a man we met at one of our seminars.

John lived by this simple adage: "Never go anywhere without your tools." If the family was packing for a vacation, John was packing his tools. While the rest of the family bustled about the house finding suitcases and suntan lotion, John was in the garage.

"You aren't bringing your tools again, are you?" his wife, Melinda, would ask, often while single-handedly packing clothes for each of their three children.

John would look more hurt than shocked at that question. It was truly inconceivable to him that his wife would question his need for tools on a vacation. "Of course," he would answer. "I don't go anywhere without my tools. You know that."

"But, dear, we're flying this time," she observed before one vacation. "I don't think you'll need your tools in Florida."

John had to brace himself against his upright tool chest to keep from falling over in disbelief. "That's *exactly* why I need my tools," he said. He locked eyes with hers, trying to connect at a new and deeper level than ever before. "The rental car certainly won't have tools. What if something happens?"

"What if it's too heavy to take on the plane?"

"I'm not taking the entire chest." John discreetly pushed the chest back into its place against the garage wall. "I'm . . . I'm taking a smaller chest. It'll be my carry-on bag."

John watched his wife's eyes roll back in her head, and because she did not suffer from seizures, he assumed she was merely expressing disbelief.

GUY FACT

Male monkeys lose the hair on their heads in the same manner men do.

Anyway, he took the tools. And the fact that no tool-type emergency arose on that vacation was—by John's assessment—a direct result of his having his tools around.

Just in case.

So it came as no surprise to John that the time he actually needed his tools on a family vacation was the one and only time he forgot them.

It was a short trip, really. A three-hour drive from the family's home near Portland, Oregon, to an island getaway outside Seattle. They were halfway to Seattle when John gasped and felt the distinct rush of blood leaving his face. Something was missing!

"Oh, no!" He shouted, both hands gripping the steering wheel.

His wife had been sleeping, but his words caused her to sit bolt upright. Later she explained that a million terrible thoughts raced through her mind in that instant. They were about to be hit by another car. . . . John was having a heart attack. . . . They'd forgotten one of the children. . . . He'd run over a dog.

Something terrible. Something drastic.

"John!" She was breathless, her heart racing. "What is it?"

"I can't believe this. . . . " He shot her a look, and when she saw the squint in his eyes, she wondered whether she could handle the gravity of the problem. He raked his fingers through his hair, and his hand shook as he set it back on the wheel. "I forgot my tools," he announced.

She stared at him for a long time, and John had the distinct feeling she did not understand the situation. "Your tools?" she asked incredulously.

"Yes. I never go anywhere without my tools. You know that."

Melinda had no sympathy whatsoever. She grabbed her pillow from the backseat, folded it beneath her head, and went back to sleep.

But John knew they were in trouble. Big trouble. He knew that the law of averages states that most mechanical breakdowns occur when a man forgets his tools. And sure enough, they were getting in line for the ferryboat when he heard a strange tapping sound coming from the engine.

"Oh, no!" John looked at Melinda again.

This time she nodded the same way she often nodded at the children. "Yes, dear, I know. You forgot your tools."

"No, it's the engine."

At that moment, the car sputtered like an octogenarian finishing a seven-hour marathon. In less than ten seconds, the engine was dead.

There they were. The entire family stuck in a ferryboat line, their car engine dead.

And not a single tool.

John climbed out of the car, lifted the hood, and stared at the sorry engine. Mere words could not describe the feeling of utter helplessness John felt at that moment. He could see what was wrong. He even knew which tools he needed to fix it. But every tool he owned was back at home in his garage.

At that very instant, an eighteen-wheeler pulled up on the opposite side of the road. The driver got out and walked up to John. "Everything okay?"

"Not really." John explained the situation with the engine. "And get this . . . I forgot my tools at home."

"No!"

"Yes!" John shook his head. "I've never felt so stupid."

To hear Melinda tell the story later, John might as well have told the trucker he forgot his wife and children at home. Immediately the trucker's reaction went from amazement to empathy.

"Well, I've got a toolbox with me," the man said, looking at his watch. "I'll be back through here again on Sunday night. What if I give you my tools, and when you're done just leave them at the corner gas station. I know the guys there. They'll take care of 'em until I get back."

GUY FACT

A Saudi Arabian woman can get a divorce if her husband doesn't give her coffee.

John couldn't have been more grateful if the trucker had offered to buy him a new car. He accepted the man's tools, along with a ride to and from the parts store. He spent two hours fixing the engine, and they were off. John marveled at the trucker's kindness for every one of the two hundred miles home.

"Can you believe it?" John said. "He actually *gave* me his tools . . . me, a perfect stranger. That means the trucker has no tools of his own for a whole day. A whole day!"

Not much about the trip stands out in John's mind today except the fact that he'd blundered so badly in forgetting his tools.

He has never forgotten his tools since then, because even now he remembers how awful it felt to be without them.

And that's the same way we men should feel about the essential relationship tools.

Most men have a toolbox in the garage and an adequate supply of internal tools—the tools we've been talking about. Some men even have a handful of relational tools. But nearly every man we've counseled or met needs to add at least one of the relational tools to his toolbox.

Soon we'll take a look at what relational tools you might need to add to your toolbox. But first there are a few important facts we want to make clear.

IMPORTANT FACT #1: GOD DOES NOT MAKE MISTAKES

Some of you guys might wonder why you need to add one or more of the relational tools when you were created in God's image. God created us for relationships, right? So why didn't he equip us with the proper tools? The answer is this: We are all sinners. And over time we men were drawn to the things we excelled at—providing and protecting—while women were drawn to the things *they* excelled at—relationships.

This doesn't mean there are no men with relationship tools, and it doesn't mean women can't head up a corporation. What it means is that, in general, when our toolboxes lack something, it is usually the relational tools. Not because God didn't hand them out, but because along the way we failed to take hold of them and learn to use them. Many of us guys gravitated toward the other internal tools, the ones that help make us good providers and protectors. God handed those out also. But in our desire to provide and protect, lots of us neglected the relational tools. It's a balance issue, and it's one you'll want to fix when it comes to building relationships.

IMPORTANT FACT #2: RELATIONAL BUILDING BENEFITS YOU TOO

Let's be honest. Lots of you guys are reading this book because someone you love thinks you're lousy at relating. Good for you for picking it up! But we want to let you in on a little secret. Building great relationships not only benefits loved ones; it benefits you as well. It gives you a deep sense of emotional well-being, it improves your stress level, and it improves your physical health and longevity.[1]

Okay, that said, let's take a look at the list of relational tools you might need to add to your internal toolbox. These are the six relational tools we will focus on for the remainder of this book:

✗ Open-sharing tool
✗ Patient-listening tool
✗ Win-win tool
✗ Selfless-honor tool
✗ Tender-touch tool
✗ Time-and-energy tool

Let's do a quick review of the reason we need tools—literal ones *and* internal ones. It's because we're trying to build or repair something, right? When we reach for the tools in the garage, we have a shelf to hang or a door to fix. Gavin had cobwebs to clear, and Ed had a swing set to build. The bottom line is this: When we have a job to do, we need to reach for the right tool for the job.

The same is true when it comes to protecting and providing. We can grab the fact-finding tool or the take-charge tool and conquer nearly any work-related situation.

TOOL TIP

All six of the relational tools can help you in your relationships, but there is a time and place to use each one of them.

For that reason, when it comes to building relationships, we must understand the task at hand. Take a look at the relational projects listed in the chart on the next page, and determine what you're trying to build. Believe us, knowing what you're trying to build and which tool to use will make all the difference later on in this book when we take you shopping for those relational tools.

Think about the last time you used your literal tools to build or repair something. Most projects take a handful of tools to complete, but there is always a key tool, a tool that is absolutely crucial to the task at hand.

The same is true with relationships.

Obviously a rewarding engagement will require you to use every one of the relational tools. For example, it is unthinkable that you might spend that time with your future wife without using the open-sharing tool. Hopes and dreams, expectations and lessons learned must all be shared during an engagement.

Of course, open sharing doesn't stop with the wedding vows. A lifelong, enjoyable marriage requires the use of the patient-listening tool too. But in marriage it is essential that you also have a grip on the selfless-honor tool and the tender-touch tool.

Remember this: All relationship-building projects require a relational toolbox.

RELATIONSHIP-BUILDING PROJECTS	TOOLS NEEDED
A successful dating relationship	Patient-listening tool
A rewarding engagement	Open-sharing tool
A lifelong, enjoyable marriage	Selfless-honor tool, tender-touch tool
A lasting friendship	Time-and-energy tool
A positive working relationship	Win-win tool
A strong sibling or parent relationship	Selfless-honor tool
An effective parental relationship	Patient-listening tool, tender-touch tool

You will need to pull out one of the relational tools in nearly every successful relationship you build, and many relationships will require using all the tools in the box. But there are key tools for each one, and those are listed above.

How important is it that we grasp this?

Crucial.

Because when we use the wrong relational tool, we wind up with the same kind of trouble Delbert and his friend had a few years ago.

The Trouble with Using the Wrong Tool

We ran into Delbert at a seminar we held one July in the deep South.

That summer was particularly muggy in the Southern town where Delbert and his buddy Dan lived. Both men were in construction and knew a great deal about tools. In fact, if there were a line of guys who understand the importance of using the right tool, Delbert and Dan would be near the front.

When Saturday arrived and Delbert and Dan decided to go duck hunting, neither of them was thinking tools. They were thinking ducks. Delbert said later he was actually thinking roasted duck.

They were sitting along the shores of a lesser-known lake, enjoying a whisper-like breeze rarely felt in the South's summer months. Suddenly Delbert saw something move.

This could have been a good thing if the moving object had been floating on or flying near the lake. However, this moving item was crawling on the ground not far from Delbert's boot.

"Yikes!" he shouted, in as manly a tone as he could muster.

Herein lay a secret about Delbert: he hated bugs. Not just poisonous spiders or gushy garden slugs. All bugs. The bigger the bug, the deeper seated Delbert's fear. Until that morning, Dan didn't know this. Alerted by his friend's shout, Dan glanced down and immediately saw the problem.

It was a centipede, marching its many pairs of feet directly toward Delbert.

Now, many of you may think a centipede is nothing more than a worm with too many legs. This isn't exactly true—especially in some parts of the country. This centipede was eight inches long and had, in Dan's words, a distinctively evil look on its face.

"Evil," he told us at the conference. "Definitely evil. You could see his eyes. They were hard. Like flint."

The centipede was somewhat raised up, towering an inch or two off the ground as it moved in for the attack. Dan realized certain things right off. First, Delbert was clearly paralyzed with fear. And second, Dan couldn't let a centipede conquer his friend without doing something about it.

So, grasping his task-oriented, take-charge, and problem-solving tools all at once, Dan shouted, "Stand back!"

In his panic, Delbert took this to mean "Stand up!" which he did. Dan stood up at the same time, so they were now side by side, standing over the centipede.

As quickly as his reflexes would move, Dan pointed his .22 caliber rifle at the centipede and fired.

Bang! The gun went off, immediately obliterating the centipede and spraying dozens of small hairy legs onto both Delbert's and Dan's pants. But neither of them noticed because the centipede's body wasn't quite enough to absorb the bullet. After pulverizing the centipede, the bullet—still moving at a considerable rate—ricocheted off a rock on the ground and squarely into Delbert's forehead!

GUY FACT
The average total spending for a formal wedding is $17,470.

Delbert—who had originally been afraid of an evil-eyed centipede, which even in its most terrifying position stood only two or three inches tall—was now bleeding profusely from the forehead.

Dan helped his friend to the car, where Delbert passed out en route to the hospital.

Thankfully, this outdoor adventure had a happy ending. Skilled doctors removed the bullet from Delbert's skull, stitched up his forehead, and sent him on his way.

"I think maybe a rifle was too powerful a tool for the centipede," Dan explained in the emergency room.

We agree.

In the same way, even the best relational tools must be used at appropriate times. For example, when your wife wants to be heard, it is usually not time to apply the tender-touch tool. And when she wants to be held, the open-sharing tool is probably better saved for another time.

Even worse, of course, is when we use one of our internal tools in place of a relational tool. Use the take-charge tool in a situation that calls for tender touch, and you'll find yourself not much better off than Delbert—stumbling around with a headache, wondering what went wrong.

Using the right tool is the key to building good relationships. The trouble is, most men try to construct their relationship projects using the internal tools we discussed earlier.

WARNING:
Do not attempt to build relationships with your internal provider/protector tools.

THE RIGHT TOOL AT THE RIGHT TIME

The following chart shows not only what women want but also the internal tools a man tends to reach for in a given situation. Finally, it will tell you which relational tool you'll need if you want to get the job done right.

WHAT MOST WOMEN WANT	THE NATURAL INTERNAL TOOL	THE BETTER RELATIONAL TOOL
To hear intimate, personal details	Fact-giving tool	Open-sharing tool
To be heard and understood at a deep level	Fact-finding tool	Patient-listening tool
To feel like an equal, respected partner	Take-charge tool	Win-win tool
To have their needs understood and appreciated	Task-oriented tool	Selfless-honor tool
To be touched and physically affirmed when they are hurting or troubled	Problem-solving tool	Tender-touch tool
To connect through shared activity	Competitive-drive tool	Time-and-energy tool

We once counseled a couple—Bill and Barb—who struggled to relate to each other. Originally Barb's struggles with a key friendship caused the problems. A woman Barb had known all her life had betrayed her and turned her back on their friendship.

"Barb was upset about this for weeks," Bill explained. "She was down and discouraged, crying all the time. The whole thing seemed a little excessive."

Now, a conflict like this offers valuable opportunities for building a better marriage—a closer, deeper, and more trusting relationship. Instead, the conflict between Barb and her friend tore down the foundation of her marriage with Bill at an alarming rate.

Here's the reason: Every time Barb was upset about her friendship, Bill moved in with his internal provider/protector tools. "This is ridiculous," he'd tell her, hammering her with his take-charge tool. "She couldn't be a good friend if she treats you this way."

Barb would cry harder. "You don't understand. I've known her all my life."

Out came Bill's problem-solving tool: "Then maybe it's time to let her go. You don't need a friend like that."

And so it went.

Bill might as well have been aiming a rifle at a centipede.

Take a look at this list, and see what can happen when a man uses his internal provider/protector tools in relational situations:

✗ Hurt feelings and hopelessness
✗ Frustration and anger
✗ Arguments and misunderstanding
✗ Betrayal and broken relationships
✗ Hard-heartedness and divorce

In counseling this couple, we helped Bill see that he needed to use different relational tools in his situation with Barb. We explained it to Bill this way.

Barb is sitting on the sofa, her head in her hands, weeping over the loss of her friendship. Bill might sort through his repertoire of new relational tools and pull out the win-win tool.

"I'm sorry you're hurting, honey," Bill could say, taking a seat beside her. "Have you considered talking to your friend, meeting for lunch maybe?"

"She doesn't want to meet," Barb might say, her tears coming harder than before. "My best friend in the world thinks I've changed."

Sensing that there is little he can say to help this situation, Bill could reach into his relational toolbox and pull out the tender-touch tool. Placing a gentle hand on Barb's shoulder, he might pull her close and give her arm soothing strokes until she stops crying. A simple—not seductive—kiss on her cheek could go well with the following words: "No matter what happens with her, I'll always be here for you, Barb. You know that, right?"

Bill began to use his relational tools at home, and over time his and Barb's marriage troubles began to subside. Barb's friendship troubles didn't go away immediately. But the conflict with Barb's friend provided this couple with valuable building materials. Once Bill understood the importance of having and using relational tools, he was able to take a difficult situation and make his marriage stronger.

We're generalizing here, but we'll go out on a limb and say that men want to be successful. Not just in the workplace but in every situation. It's part of our internal makeup, the reason we have the natural internal tools we've already discussed.

But if we're going to be successful in relationships, we *must* fill our toolbox with the right relational tools. And we must remember that relational tools are subtle. That's right, subtle. And since most men feel comfortable with the take-charge and competitive-drive tools, it's important that this point is clear. Why? Because men do not often venture into the subtle without making a determined decision to do so.

Most guys will use their internal provider/protector tools with a great deal of gusto and sometimes forceful behavior. This is not the way we want to use our relational tools. If we do, then it is possible our greatest intentions will backfire.

Here we are reminded of Ted, a man we met at a seminar.

Ted didn't live near the Ozarks, but he had a spider problem all the same. Ted's problem was the infamous black widow spider. And not just the black widow but also cockroaches and an occasional scorpion.

Ted lived in Arizona, where he and his wife had purchased two acres of desert land, which they later learned was crawling with creepy critters. This didn't bother Ted, really, because the kinds of creepy critters that found their way inside his home rarely came out in broad daylight. And since Ted was a sound sleeper, he figured it would work okay to live and let live where the critters were concerned.

GUY FACT

In the marriage ceremony of the ancient Incas, the couple was considered officially wed when they took off their sandals and handed them to each other.

Ted's wife, Sue, however, did not feel this way.

One night Sue woke up sometime after midnight with a dry throat. She tiptoed delicately downstairs for a glass, but when she turned on the light, she heard a skittering noise that sounded like a troop of ballet dancers exiting the stage. Only this wasn't a theater; it was a brand-new kitchen. And the skittering came not from slippered feet but from an entire army of cockroaches.

Sue screamed and dropped her glass. Neither sound woke Ted, but the next morning Sue explained the problem.

"Make more noise when you get up," Ted suggested. "That way, you'll never see 'em."

The huff that came from Sue's throat was memorable.

Now, you men who've been paying attention will notice that Ted used his problem-solving tool. But really in this situation we'd suggest first using the tender-touch tool, then the selfless-honor tool. Give a gentle touch on the shoulder or a comforting hug, followed by a promise to do something about the bugs. Remember, this type of solution benefits both people in the relationship.

But Ted was bent on making things work his way.

Another week passed, and one day Sue came home from the grocery store to find a scorpion tap-dancing on her kitchen counter. As she turned to run from the house, a wasp dive-bombed her from his resting place on the ceiling. Sue looked up, and there it was: the beginnings of a wasp nest anchored to the side of the light fixture.

That was, as Sue tells it, the final straw. She went back outside and sat in her car until Ted got home.

Ted had worked hard that day. He was intent on getting inside, pouring himself a glass of iced tea, and kicking back in his recliner. But even fixated on such a task, Ted couldn't help but notice the fact that Sue was sitting in her car, the windows down only an inch or two.

"Sue?" He approached the car nervously.

"I'm not getting out, Ted!" She rolled the window down another few inches. "There are cockroaches and scorpions and wasps in that house. Either do something about them or I'm leaving."

Ted looked over his shoulder at the house. Wasn't this supposed to be their dream house? He glanced back at Sue and blinked. "Where will you go?"

"Ted!" Sue's voice sounded like a roller coaster screaming its way downhill. "I'm serious! I'll be at my sister's house until you make things safe."

Sue started the car, backed out (very nearly over Ted's feet), and disappeared down the dusty desert road. Ted was left standing there, still hankering for a glass of iced tea but with Sue's words echoing hard in the hallways of his mind.

Make things safe. . . .

Yes! That was it! He had another task now, a problem to solve. He climbed back in his car, and an hour later he was back with two bug foggers. He set them off, left the house, and found Sue at her sister's place. The next day he ventured back and was stunned to find things worse than he'd left them.

"There were actually cockroaches partying on the living-room rug," Ted said. "It was pitiful."

If two foggers weren't the answer, Ted had another idea. Ten miles out of town was a chemical warehouse that sold bulk amounts to the public. Ted drove out and approached a man at the warehouse office.

"I need a deal on foggers," Ted explained.

The man nodded, understanding Ted's problem. "I can sell you a pallet. They're expired, but they work."

"How many in a pallet?"

"Three hundred."

The man gave Ted a price, and immediately Ted figured out that it was less than he would have to pay for ten foggers at the hardware store. "Sold!" Ted smiled, and in an hour he loaded the pallet on his pickup truck, brought it home, and placed the foggers around his house.

Now, when Ted says he placed three hundred foggers around his house, he means around, over, and through his house. The house was literally covered with foggers. No point in saving some of the foggers for later. After all, they were expired and probably only half the strength of nonexpired foggers. Besides, a onetime super treatment was bound to solve the problem.

He set fifty across his living room, thirty in each bedroom, and another fifty in a trail along the inside perimeter walls. Seventy-five foggers polka-dotted the kitchen counters and floor. Then, moving like Wile E. Coyote on a mission, Ted darted through the house setting off the foggers.

This'll take care of those bugs, he hummed happily to himself.

And perhaps the story would have had a relatively uneventful ending—other than placing Ted's single-story house on the map as the only U.S. toxic waste site with bedrooms—except for one thing. He placed a few foggers a bit too close to the gas stove. The chemicals released into the air danced dangerously with the pilot light and . . .

Bam! An explosion rang through Ted's brand-new house, blowing out the windows, lifting the roof three inches off the walls, and causing second-degree burns on Ted's hands and face.

Ted dashed outside, running for his life, and fell flat down on the desert ground, where he passed out, overcome by fogger fumes. A neighbor heard the explosion and called 911, bringing an ambulance and fire truck to the scene. They fitted Ted with an oxygen mask, and—wearing protective breathing apparatuses—they spent thirty minutes scouring Ted's home and defusing foggers.

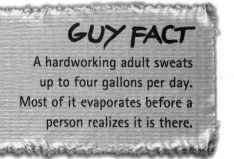

GUY FACT

A hardworking adult sweats up to four gallons per day. Most of it evaporates before a person realizes it is there.

Paramedics took Ted to the hospital where, two days later, his battered lungs and burned body parts were well enough for him to be released.

"I'll have only a few scars when I'm totally healed," Ted told us. He still had a bandage on his forehead. "I guess three hundred foggers were a few too many."

We had to agree.

But get this: Ted's wife—once she got over the $50,000 in damages to the new house—was actually rather proud of Ted.

"He was trying to make me happy," she told people after the incident. "At least my safety mattered to him."

And the good news was that the foggers worked! Four weeks later, when the toxic fumes had been aired out and housing repairs completed, Ted and Sue returned to their home to find piles of dead bugs not only in their house but as far as fifty feet out into the front and back yards. And not just dead bugs, but dead weeds and grass as well. The fact that Ted and Sue may never be able to grow a garden near their home is a small inconvenience when weighed against this reality: Sue feels safe in her home, and she has Ted to thank.

Now, we know at least a few of you men are thinking Ted was maybe not the sharpest knife in the drawer. But really, guys, aren't we all a little like Ted sometimes? Taking charge, solving problems, barging our way into a situation when the subtler approach would have worked fine?

The point is, relational building requires special tools and a definite understanding of subtlety.

So what exactly does it mean to be subtle? And if relational tools are subtle, how can we see the results of what we're building? If there were a relational tool buyer's guide, it might offer these suggestions:

✗ Remember to practice.
✗ Don't expect results to be instantaneous.
✗ Allow yourself an occasional mistake.
✗ Remember, there is nothing scientific about relational tools. A hammer might always drive in a nail, but relational tools will yield differing results.
✗ Seek help from other men.

Take a look at that last item. Seek help from other men. If you're like us, you know one or two men who have this whole relational toolbox thing down. They're experts at the relational tools and are constantly looking for ways to use them more efficiently.

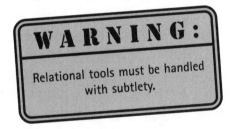

WARNING: Relational tools must be handled with subtlety.

That reminds us of Rolando, a man we met at a conference last year. Rolando was simply amazing with tools. He wasn't an electrician or plumber, and he didn't make his living in construction. In fact, he worked in the state corrections department. But people from a dozen different state departments would bring their tired and broken things to Rolando with full faith that he'd find a way to fix them.

The more solid Rolando's credibility grew, the more things people brought for him to fix. Eventually they brought broken items straight to his house. This, in turn, caused Rolando's neighbors to take note of his special talent with tools.

Rolando told us about the time the guy next door brought a broken lawn mower over. Like children at a circus, half a dozen other men in the neighborhood stopped their yard work and Saturday chores and found their way to Rolando's garage.

"Before I knew it, I was working on the lawn mower with eight guys gathered around me," Rolando told us.

"You don't care if we watch, do you?" one of the guys asked.

"No, go ahead," Rolando said as he wheeled his towering tool chest over toward the lawn mower. "It won't take me long."

The men watched, mesmerized. Here was a man who not only had the right tools for just about any job, but he also knew how to use them. And that was something worth giving up an hour of a Saturday to see. In fact, every man there admitted to Rolando a desire to learn more about using tools by watching Rolando in action.

It's the same way with our relational tools. Think about men who have the relational tools and know how to use them. Then make a plan to spend more time with those men. Talk to them about their relationships, ask them about open sharing and patient listening and the other tools.

You never know. Before long the crowd of men might just be gathered around you.

THE IMPORTANCE OF BUILDING STRONG RELATIONSHIPS

World-famous cardiologist Dr. Dean Ornish says anything that promotes a sense of isolation leads to illness and suffering. And anything that promotes a sense of love, intimacy, connection, openness, and community is healing.[2]

Remember those internal tools we talked about at the beginning of this book? They are wonderful for providing and protecting. But remember that if using them leads to independence, to disconnection from others, you'll wind up with problems. You must keep a healthy balance.

At the same time, if you're willing to add the six basic relational tools to your toolbox, you'll find that you will feel better than ever about your relationships.

Now that you understand those tools a little better, grab your toolbox. It's time to do a little shopping. Remember, adding relational tools to your toolbox is not an exact science. But as you read the next chapter, you'll become more familiar with the key relational tools, familiar enough to understand what you're trying to build and which tool might work best in that situation. That way you never have to hurt someone you love by reaching for the wrong tool. And that's an important bit of information.

Just ask Dan and Delbert.

Adding to Your Relational Toolbox: One-Stop Shopping

We know men who make a regular weekly trip to Home Depot. And why not? The place is the tool man's paradise, the one-stop shopping center for every possible kind of project.

In fact, next time you're at Home Depot or any other such store, stop and watch the men streaming down the aisles. You'll see that they are driven and excited, eager to buy their tools and even more eager to get them home and use them.

That's how we guys should be when it comes to shopping for relational tools.

Now let's take the Home Depot analogy a step further. When we guys buy a new tool at Home Depot, we have some options when it comes to learning how to use it. We can read the instructions, ask someone who knows how to use it, take a class at the local hardware store, watch a demonstration video, or use trial and error.

None of these options is wrong. In fact, you'll probably rely on most of them at one time or another in the course of mastering the use of that tool.

The same is true with our relational tools. We'll talk in this chapter about the one-stop shopping place for relational tools, and then later we'll take a closer look at how we can learn to use them. Stay with us, now. The best stuff is just ahead.

Let's take a look at the ultimate one-stop shopping center for relational tools: the Bible.

GOD'S WORD—THE HOME DEPOT OF RELATIONAL TOOLS

If you want to add relational tools to your toolbox, the first thing you should do is grab a Bible. Between the covers of this book lies all the truth you'll need to equip yourself with these relational tools as well as learn to use them in your own relationships.

Here is an example of what can happen when a man "goes shopping" for relational tools in the Bible.

Mark's wife had two complaints about him: He never shared his feelings, and he never listened to her. But Mark is a living example of the truth of Scripture when it comes to the promise that nothing is impossible with God.

After exploring the relational tools found in the Bible, Mark was a changed man. His wife now has a favorite verse, one that you may want to rely on: "[Jesus] even makes the deaf hear and the mute speak" (Mark 7:37).

So there you have it. Jesus is the miracle worker. He's the one who will hand you deaf guys the tools to listen and you "one-word wonders" the tools to finally open your mouths and speak.

On that note, grab your toolbox. Let's pop inside the storehouse of God's Word and get down to business.

THE OPEN-SHARING TOOL

The open-sharing tool is vital to any good relationship because it helps us guys talk. It helps us talk about the small details of our lives, explore our motives, and articulate our feelings. All of these "skills" can help us relate better to the people we love.

You think talking to your loved ones is our idea? Think again!

Let's take a trip back through time to a very important supper—the one Jesus shared with his followers the night before he was crucified.

Take a minute to get this picture in your head: Here's Jesus, knowing full well that he's about to be crucified, and his attention is entirely on his followers.

Had Jesus been an ordinary, average man, the conversation between him and the disciples that night could have gone like this:

"So what's the party for, Jesus?"

"Oh, nothing. I just thought it'd be nice to get together."

"Okay. But how are you? You look, I don't know, troubled somehow."

"No, everything's fine. Just a long day."

"Really? Are you sure?"

"Yep. Will someone pass the grapes?"

But Jesus understood the art of open sharing. He, better than any of them at the table that night, knew what was ahead—what terrible, dark moments lay just around the corner. And because he loved his friends, he shared with them. Not one-word answers, but deep thoughts, straight from his heart.

Eavesdrop with us on some of the things Jesus shared that evening, and you'll see what we mean:

✗ "I have eagerly desired to eat this Passover with you before I suffer" (Luke 22:15).
✗ "For I tell you, I will not eat it again until it finds fulfillment in the kingdom of God" (v. 16).
✗ "I am among you as one who serves" (v. 27).
✗ "You are those who have stood by me in my trials" (v. 28).
✗ "I have prayed for you, Simon, that your faith may not fail" (v. 32).
✗ "What is written about me is reaching its fulfillment" (v. 37).

Jesus was troubled in spirit, to the point that a few hours later he would sweat drops of blood. But at the supper, his concern was for his disciples, for sharing with them some final things from his heart. Of course, this was only the last in a series of countless times Jesus shared with his disciples. He regularly told them of his love for them and did everything possible to let them know he cared.

TOOL TIP

Every internal tool you will need to build or repair your relationships is found in the written Word of God, the Bible.

Jesus was the inventor of the open-sharing tool. You can obtain this tool at no cost by becoming a student of Jesus—by reading about him in the Gospels and by reading what his followers said about him in their letters. As you do that, take note of the times and opportunities when the Lord used this relational tool.

Here are some other Scripture passages that talk about the importance of the open-sharing tool:

- ✗ "Do not let any unwholesome talk come out of your mouths, but only what is helpful for building others up according to their needs, that it may benefit those who listen" (Ephesians 4:29).
- ✗ "Let us consider how we may spur one another on toward love and good deeds" (Hebrews 10:24).
- ✗ "Let us not give up meeting together, as some are in the habit of doing, but let us encourage one another—and all the more as you see the Day approaching" (Hebrews 10:25).
- ✗ "Dear friends, let us love one another, for love comes from God. Everyone who loves has been born of God and knows God" (1 John 4:7).

Now it's time to pick up the next relational tool on your shopping list. Let's move over one aisle, about halfway down. There it is!

THE PATIENT-LISTENING TOOL

The patient-listening tool makes listening a priority in our relationships. It helps us hear not just words but also the meaning behind the words. It helps us take a genuine interest in what our loved ones are saying.

We are convinced that for many of us men, patient listening is one of the most difficult tools to add to our toolbox. Why? Because often we don't see the need for what we consider excessive dialogue.

Certainly Jesus had every human reason to feel this way. After all, he already knew what was going to happen next. Besides that, he was a busy man with incredible tasks before him. But that didn't stop him from being an amazing listener.

Take a look at the story of Lazarus's death, for instance. Still a long way from Lazarus's house, Jesus is bombarded with grief-stricken friends. First Martha runs to him, then Mary. They want to talk to Jesus, and their message is basically the same: "Our brother is dead, and you could have done something to stop it!"

Jesus could have told these people to stop complaining or simply reminded them that he had things under control. He could have chided them for their lack of faith or just told them he was too busy to listen to their crying.

Remember, Jesus knows the outcome. He knows that Lazarus will rise again. And when Martha and Mary run to him—complaining and distraught—Jesus patiently, kindly tells them, "Your brother will rise again."

Martha basically tells Jesus, "Yeah, yeah, yeah . . . at the end of the age that'll happen, but not now. Here, today, our brother is dead, and I'm upset about it!"

Jesus doesn't mock or belittle her. Instead, after patiently listening, he reminds her of who he is: "I am the resurrection and the life. He who believes in me will live, even though he dies; and whoever lives and believes in me will never die. Do you believe this?" (John 11:25-26).

Still listening, the group travels down the road to the house where the sisters lived with Lazarus. Now it's Mary's turn: "Lord, if you had been here, my brother would not have died" (v. 32).

Again, Jesus would be justified in giving any number of responses. But instead, he says nothing. He looks at Mary and the others, all of them weeping, and is deeply moved. The Scriptures don't tell us how long Jesus stood there before he spoke. Maybe he put a hand on Mary's shoulder or locked eyes with her for a long moment. He felt her pain because he had listened to her. And not just to her words but to her heart's plaintive cry.

Jesus simply asks, "Where have you laid him?" (v. 34).

The people led Jesus to the tomb, and once more he demonstrates the patient-listening tool. An entire village is mourning the loss of this wonderful friend and brother. And Jesus, standing in their midst, staring at a tomb, hears them so well that he cries right along with them. Here, recorded in one of our favorite Scripture verses, is Jesus' response to his friends' grief: "Jesus wept" (v. 35).

Jesus had patiently, carefully, kindly listened to his friends in their darkest, direst hour. He did not shout at them or roll his eyes. Instead, he listened to them and cried with them.

Again, there are ample illustrations of Jesus' exhibiting this type of behavior throughout the New Testament. Spend time in the Gospels awhile, and you'll see plenty of times when Jesus used his patient-listening tool. These passages also give you references to patient listening. Think of them as aisles in the greatest Home Depot of all.

✗ "Be kind and compassionate to one another, forgiving each other, just as in Christ God forgave you" (Ephesians 4:32).
✗ "All of you should be of one mind, full of sympathy toward each other, loving one another with tender hearts and humble minds" (1 Peter 3:8, NLT).
✗ "Carry each other's burdens, and in this way you will fulfill the law of Christ" (Galatians 6:2).
✗ "Remind your people to . . . be gentle and show true humility to everyone" (Titus 3:1-2, NLT).
✗ "Everyone should be quick to listen, slow to speak and slow to become angry" (James 1:19).

Now it's time to move on to the next relational tool on our shopping list. We'll find this tool in a section of the store that's been around a lot longer than the others we've visited so far.

THE WIN-WIN TOOL

Many, if not most, men need to add the win-win tool to their relational toolboxes. This tool helps us to set our own desires aside and give in to our loved ones' desires more often. It also helps us to value their opinions and how they think.

Let's take a step further back in time for this bit of shopping—back to Old Testament times. Jesus constantly taught about compromise that results in a win-win situation, but a section of Old Testament Scripture gives us a wonderful example of the win-win tool in action.

Journey with us back to the days of Abraham. Genesis 13:5-18 tells the story of Abraham and Lot, and it gives us a demonstration of the win-win tool.

God had asked Abraham to leave his home, his people, and his land to travel to a faraway and unfamiliar place. That might not be so hard today, what with trains, planes, and automobiles. But back then it meant moving thousands of livestock, herdsmen, and their families, and who knows how many tents. We're talking donkey and camel travel at this point, so *slow* doesn't even begin to describe it.

Lot was Abraham's nephew, so he tagged along the way relatives tend to do. Lot also had flocks and herds and herdsmen, and this massive group trekked across the desert together. Things were as plucky as the first day of a family reunion until the group heard something in the distance.

It turned out to be the unwelcome sound of people fighting—in this case, Lot's people against Abraham's people. The problem soon became clear enough: The land wasn't big enough to support the groups of both men. No one could see a solution, and the uproar grew until Abraham stepped forward and cleared his throat.

"Look," he said. "Let's not fight. I mean, come on, we're family, right?"

Lot stood there, unblinking. And that's when Abraham reached for the win-win tool.

"Tell you what," Abraham said, and gave his nephew a friendly smile and a pat on the back. "Looks like the party's over, but I'll give you first dibs on the land thing. If you wanna go right, I'll go left. You go left, I'll go right. Whatever makes you happy."

Now, we might add here that if Lot had grabbed the win-win tool himself, he might have hesitated and said something like, "No, no . . . by all means, this is your journey, after all. You choose first."

But Lot didn't say anything of the sort. Instead, he grinned like a lottery winner and took the well-watered land of the Jordan. Abraham got what was left.

We can just see you guys, mouths agape, stunned at how unfair this was to Abraham. But fear not. God saw Abraham's heart as surely as he will see yours when you wield the win-win tool with your loved one.

In the end, God pulled Abraham aside and said, "Lift up your eyes from where you are and look north and south, east and west. All the land that you see I will give to you and your offspring forever" (Genesis 13:14-15).

See that? God took care of Abraham, and he'll take care of you. Just make sure you have that win-win tool in your toolbox. And while you're at it, check out these Scripture passages:

✗ "Get rid of all bitterness, rage and anger, brawling and slander, along with every form of malice" (Ephesians 4:31).
✗ "Be imitators of God, therefore, as dearly loved children and live a life of love, just as Christ loved us and gave himself up for us as a fragrant offering and sacrifice to God" (Ephesians 5:1).
✗ "As God's chosen people, holy and dearly loved, clothe yourselves with compassion, kindness, humility, gentleness and patience. Bear with each other and forgive whatever grievances you may have against one another. Forgive as the Lord forgave you. And over all these virtues put on love, which binds them all together in perfect unity" (Colossians 3:12-14).
✗ "Live in harmony with one another" (Romans 12:16).

Okay, guys. Now we're on the downhill side of this relational shopping spree. Just three more tools to go, and we don't have to move out of the Genesis section of the relational tool store to grab the next one.

THE SELFLESS-HONOR TOOL

The selfless-honor tool gives us men the ability to think of others first, to see the worth of our loved ones. It also aids us in giving compliments, something that never hurts in our relationships.

Here's an Old Testament example of the selfless-honor tool in action.

Joseph was one of God's favorite guys. He had lots of skills and talents, but none of them was as effective as his use of the selfless-honor tool. There's no doubt that the greatest act of selfless honor took place on Calvary, where Christ was crucified for your sins and ours. But Joseph wasn't God in the flesh. He was just a guy like you and me—a guy with a bunch of unfair duties and people around him who didn't like him.

The funny thing is, it didn't start that way for Joseph. In fact, out of a bevy of brothers, he was the favorite son. Some of you might be able to relate to that role, but not most of us.

TOOL TIP

Make sure you use the selfless-honor tool . . . well, selflessly. Don't honor your loved one or give her compliments with selfish motives.

If you're familiar with Joseph's story, which is found in Genesis 37–45, you know that his happy beginning soon led him to a world of hurt. Why? Because his brothers were lizard green with jealousy. They sold him to a passing band of travelers because they couldn't stand the way their dad favored the boy.

We know what you're thinking: *Joseph must've hated those guys!* But, ah, read on. Amazing things happen when you use the selfless-honor tool.

Joseph found himself working for a guy named Potiphar. Working for this man made Joseph something of an expert at using the selfless-honor tool.

And where did his selflessness get him?

That's right, square in the basement of the worst dungeon in town. Joseph summed up his situation and realized he had two choices: whine and complain, or get to work. Once more he reached for the selfless-honor tool. The result? He proved his worth, and in no time he was more or less running the jail.

Just when you suspect God had forgotten about poor old Joseph, the king calls his number—something about interpreting a few dreams. The next thing you know, Joseph is helping Egypt get ready for the greatest famine of the ages.

When the famine hit, guess who ran low on food? That's right—Joseph's brothers—the same guys who sold him off in the first place. Here's where the story gets good. Joseph's brothers came to Egypt begging for a bit of lunch, and when Joseph entered the room, not one of them knew it was him.

The things any of us might have said to those nasty brothers can't be printed here. They'd wrecked Joe's life, after all. But Joseph took them in his arms and wept over them.

"Forget about it," he told them. "God had a plan for me to be here."

The brothers fell into instant shock, and they were still picking themselves up off the ground when Joseph began telling them all the ways he wanted to bless them—lots of food, lots of land, lots of treasures, and special treatment.

It was more than any of those mean old brothers could have dreamed possible. And it was all the result of Joseph's willingness to build relationships with the selfless-honor tool.

"Okay, guys," you say to us. "I don't know if I can use the selfless-honor tool in my relationships. The people I love are pretty difficult."

Well, we bet none of those people ever sold you into slavery. God honored Joseph far more than Joseph ever honored anyone else, and that's the beauty of these relational tools. Use them on others, and you'll find God himself using them on you.

Isn't that great?

Here are a few accessories that go well with the selfless-honor tool:

✗ "Submit to one another out of reverence for Christ" (Ephesians 5:21).

✗ "Honor your father and mother" (Ephesians 6:2).

✗ "Love is patient, love is kind. It does not envy, it does not boast, it is not proud. It is not rude, it is not self-seeking, it is not easily angered, it keeps no record of wrongs. . . . It always protects, always trusts, always hopes, always perseveres" (1 Corinthians 13 4-7).

✗ "Be devoted to one another in brotherly love. Honor one another above yourselves" (Romans 12:10).

Research shows what can happen if a man does not embrace the selfless-honor tool and instead reacts in anger, impatience, and hostility. Renowned cardiologist Dean Ornish, author of *Love and Survival*, cites forty-five studies in which the research points to an astounding connection between hostility—a lack of selfless honor—and coronary heart disease. In each study hostility proved to be one of the most important variables in this type of heart condition.

He says, "The effects of hostility are equal or greater in magnitude to the traditional factors for heart disease, elevated cholesterol level, high blood pressure, etc. I believe hostility is a manifestation of a more fundamental issue, loneliness and isolation. People who feel lonely and isolated are often angry, causing them to feel even more lonely and isolated in a vicious cycle."[1]

You can see how a lack of selfless honor can put distance in your relationships. This, then, will increase a person's chances of suffering a major disease.

Okay, guys. We can see it from here: the end of this shopping spree. Let's head back to the days of Jesus and pick up the next relational tool the Bible has to offer.

THE TENDER-TOUCH TOOL

We probably don't have to spend a lot of time defining the tender-touch tool, do we? This tool helps us know the value of a simple hug, embrace, or other kinds of touch. While we should never confuse tender touch with sexual touch of any kind, this relational tool can help us expand our definition of a physical relationship.

TOOL TIP

Don't equate the use of tender touch with sensual or sexual touch.

It's easy for some of us guys to get kind of funny about the tender-touch tool. Some of us struggle with hugging our wives enough, let alone our kids, parents, and friends. But the aisles of the Bible are chock-full of examples of people freely using the tender-touch tool.

In the New Testament we read of folks greeting one another with embraces and holy kisses. Now, we're not suggesting you go to work tomorrow and greet your buddy with a holy kiss. Please don't! But the tender-touch tool is crucially important to our personal relationships. Why? Because there's something special about the power of touch.

Hang around Jesus long enough, and you'll see him touching the eyes of the blind, the ears of the deaf, and the bodies of the lame. But the really amazing thing is that Jesus didn't touch just the beautiful people. Your children? Your wife? Your parents? These people are easy to touch. After all, you've known and loved them for years.

But imagine for a minute touching a person with leprosy.

It's easy from our comfortable, twenty-first-century recliners to imagine leprosy as sort of a bad case of olden-day hives. Nothing could be further from the truth. When a person got leprosy, he or she was given a one-way ticket out of town and left for dead. And that is exactly what happened to people who got leprosy—they died.

What did leprosy do to the unfortunate people who contracted the disease?

Picture a snowman sitting in a yard up north in the dead of winter. Now picture what happens to that snowman as the weather gradually warms over the next several weeks. See the snowman slowly melting away? That's what it was like with leprosy. A leper's skin slowly and painfully melted off his or her body, leaving tendons and ligaments and finally bones fully exposed.

Dying of leprosy was a horrific experience made worse by this single fact: It was contagious. That meant that death came in total isolation because other people could easily catch the disease from a single touch.

This was the situation for a New Testament guy we'll call Frank. Frank's life had been—by all accounts—going along pretty well, until one day he began noticing bare patches on his arms and legs. It didn't take long for a local doctor to make the diagnosis of leprosy, meaning Frank had to pack his things, bid a final farewell to his wife and kids, and head for the outskirts of town.

Enter Jesus.

Take at look at Matthew 8:1-3, and you'll find Jesus coming down from the mountain. To set the stage a little, Jesus has just finished a lengthy sermon. If Jesus had had a limited word count, he would have used his—times ten—with the Sermon on the Mount. Our guess is that he was pretty well talked out. It would have been understandable if Jesus had asked his buddies to go before him and distract the people so he could have a little rest and relaxation.

Tired, emotionally and mentally drained after all the truth he'd just revealed, Jesus walks down the mountainside followed by large crowds of people. Suddenly from out of nowhere appears a distraught and desperate Frank.

Frank's eyes are wide with fear. Tears spill down his blotchy cheeks, and he does the only thing he knows to do: He falls at the feet of Jesus and cries out, "Lord, if you are willing, you can make me clean" (Matthew 8:2).

Can you picture the scene? The traveling crowd digs in its collective heels and stops, aghast. What is this? Frank? Good old Frank has leprosy? Murmurs of pity and horror must have made their way through the crowd.

"Do you see that? Frank has leprosy!"

"No! Not Frank."

"If it could happen to Frank, it could happen to any of us."

"Whatever will become of his family?"

The only thing that silences the crowd is Frank's audacity. Imagine, someone unclean falling at the feet of someone like Jesus. Of all the nerve!

A silence falls over the area, a silence bathed in tension. The crowd freezes in place, watching, waiting. Frank hunches over, his entire life hinging on what happens next.

Jesus—tired but smiling, drained but willing, heart heavy but open to the one thing that will make a difference in the leper's life—extends tenderness to Frank.

A single loving touch.

While the crowd quietly gasps, Jesus reaches out and touches Frank. He brushes his fingers against the newly formed holes on Frank's arms. He looks deep into the man's heart, past the fear and shame, past the hopelessness to the part of Frank that never expected to be loved again.

Jesus has just finished talking to a multitude of people about things like loving their enemies, giving to the needy, not judging others, entering through the narrow gates. But the Bible says not a word about the crowd of people stepping forward to help Frank. Only Jesus is willing to reach out and touch someone with leprosy.

"I am willing," Jesus says. "Be clean!" (Matthew 8:3).

What happens next?

In as much time as it took Jesus to pat Frank on the back, the man's skin was completely restored. *Poof!* No leprosy. Just like that. Jesus takes hold of the tender-touch tool, and Frank's as good as new.

Isn't it the same in our relationships?

Your wife, daughter, son, or friend has had a hard day, and tempers are short for everyone. Give that person a hug, and what happens? Anger dissipates as quickly as Frank's illness. Why? Because the tender-touch tool is as important to the relational toolbox as sandpaper is to the carpenter. Whatever mistakes or rough edges might have been there are easily smoothed with a tender touch.

Notice three things in this story. First, Jesus recognized a hurting person when he saw one. Second, Jesus was quick to touch the man, regardless of the cost to himself. And third, through Jesus' tender touch, a man was blessed.

Think about the people in your life. Hurting or not, they need your tender touch. And if Jesus could touch a man with leprosy, believe me, you can touch the people you love. It might just change their lives.

We guys can learn more about the tender-touch tool by reading these verses:

✗ "Greet one another with a kiss of love" (1 Peter 5:14).
✗ "Jesus had compassion on them and touched their eyes. Immediately they received their sight and followed him" (Matthew 20:34).
✗ "When Jesus came into Peter's house, he saw Peter's mother-in-law lying in bed with a fever. He touched her hand and the fever left her, and she got up and began to wait on him" (Matthew 8:14-15).
✗ "His left arm is under my head, and his right arm embraces me" (Song of Solomon 2:6).

We know how you are feeling about now. All this shopping has you worn out. But take heart! We have just one more relational tool to pick up, and then we can head home.

THE TIME-AND-ENERGY TOOL

It shouldn't come as any surprise to us guys that we need to expend time and effort in order to build or repair a relationship. This is the definition of the time-and-energy tool. This relational tool helps us make time to be with someone we love. It also helps us value noncompetitive activities with our loved one simply for the joy of being together.

We Smalley guys had a lot of fun looking at Bible stories that demonstrate uses of the time-and-energy tool. Spend a few hours in the Gospels, and you'll see Jesus giving three years' worth of time and energy to his disciples. If they were caught in a boat on that stormy old

Sea of Galilee, he was there. If they were traveling from town to town healing people, there was the Lord. The night before he was to be crucified—a day that clearly would have been a classic time for Jesus to retreat to a quiet place—there was Jesus, eating with his friends, walking with his friends, teaching his friends.

Jesus understood the time-and-energy tool because God his Father invented it.

For the purpose of this section, let's allow the women to show us guys the ropes. We'll drift back in time once more, back to Ruth 1:8-18 and a couple of precious women. These were the days when judges ruled and things seemed to go from bad to worse. First Naomi's husband died; then before Naomi's family could properly mourn that loss, her sons died.

This left Naomi with two daughters-in-law—Orpah and Ruth. These young women's situation was utterly dire, so Naomi pulled them aside and told them how it was. "Not much left for you here. You might as well go home to your parents," Naomi said. "May the Lord show kindness to you, as you have shown to your dead and to me."

Here's a woman who understood the selfless-honor tool. Not only did Naomi free her daughters-in-law of their obligation to stay with her and care for her in her old age, but she blessed them in the process. "May the Lord grant that each of you will find rest in the home of another husband" (Ruth 1:9).

The moment was too sad for the women involved, and all three burst into tears. For about half a minute, Orpah joined Ruth in protesting, promising to stay with Naomi even though their husbands were dead.

Naomi wouldn't hear of it: "Go home, daughters. This old body won't be having any more sons for you."

There were more tears, but the truth is, Orpah was out the door before Naomi finished her next sentence. Ruth, though, pulled out her time-and-energy tool and made one of the most beautiful statements in Scripture: "Don't urge me to leave you or to turn back from you. Where you go I will go, and where you stay I will stay. Your people will be my people and your God my God. Where you die, I will die, and there I will be buried" (Ruth 1:16-17).

Ruth was young and lovely and widowed. But she was willing to spend the rest of her life with Naomi simply because she understood the importance of investing time and energy in the people she loved.

Whatever happened to Ruth?

A handsome guy named Boaz came along, and before you can turn a page in the Bible, he and Ruth fell in love. Two chapters down the road, and they are getting married. Who had happy tears in the back of the church? Naomi. Because she'd had a chance to witness firsthand what happens when a person invests time and energy into a relationship.

The person who makes use of the time-and-energy tool will be blessed. The same thing is true in our relationships today. We'll let Greg tell you a story.

When my eldest daughter, Taylor, was five years old, we moved into a new neighborhood. We soon discovered that our next-door neighbor had recently gone through a difficult divorce. The father had left the family, so the mom was trying to rear her four young children by herself.

Erin and I encouraged Taylor to befriend Sarah, also five years old. We hoped that the hurting child might find some comfort around our house after the pain of divorce and the loss of her father.

One day Taylor and Sarah were playing in our daughter's upstairs bedroom while I watched a football game in the family room. Erin had gone shopping.

In the middle of the game I heard a loud argument break out upstairs. Angry voices from Taylor's room kept yelling, "Yes, they will!" "No, they won't!" "Yes, they will!" "No, they won't!" It went on like that for some time. I assumed the girls were fighting over Barbie dolls or whatever else causes five-year-olds to scream at one another.

The conflict quickly spilled out into the hall, down the stairs, and finally came to rest next to my chair. I muted the TV (why miss any of the game?) and asked, "Girls, what's the problem?"

"Daddy," Taylor replied testily, "will you tell Sarah that you and mommy are *not* going to get a divorce?"

So much for Barbie!

When I recovered my wits and realized that a teachable moment had arrived, I turned off the TV and swooped both girls into my lap.

"Sarah," I gently said, "I hate to get involved in this argument, but I have to tell you that Taylor is right. Taylor's mom and I are *not* going to get a divorce. That means that I have to learn to be a great husband and father."

I had no time to savor my wise words, however, for my daughter reacted to her "victory" by sticking out her tongue at Sarah. Taylor then dashed back up to her room. Sarah didn't move.

I turned on the TV once more, and Sarah remained seated. In fact, she sat in my lap and watched the football game with me for thirty minutes. Finally, feeling a little nervous that her mother might misinterpret events if Sarah should tell her, "Momma, I sat in Dr. Smalley's lap *all afternoon!*" I made a suggestion.

"Sarah," I said, "why don't you go back up and play with Taylor?"

Obediently this precious little girl got up, started to leave, took about three steps—and then stopped. It appeared as if she wanted to say something.

"Hey, sweetie, are you all right? Is everything okay?" I asked softly.

With her chin drooping and in a voice barely above a whisper, she said: "Well, I was just thinking. Would it be okay if I came back sometime and watched football with you? I could pretend that you're my daddy."

I choked back tears as I held that little girl tightly in my arms and reassured her that I'd be lucky to have her as my football buddy. Time and energy. It's a priceless gift.

As you think about how you can use your time and energy to bless others, take a look at these Scripture passages. They assure us that this relational tool—like the others—was invented by none other than God Almighty.

✗ "A new command I give you: Love one another. As I have loved you, so you must love one another" (John 13:34).

✗ "Husbands, love your wives, just as Christ loved the church and gave himself up for her" (Ephesians 5:25).

✗ "In this same way, husbands ought to love their wives as their own bodies. He who loves his wife loves himself" (Ephesians 5:28).

✗ "Serve wholeheartedly, as if you were serving the Lord, not men" (Ephesians 6:7).

Now that you have your relational tools tucked away in your toolbox, let's talk about how you might become more adept at using them. In the following chapters we'll take a look at what we're trying to build and the ways we can become expert builders with our new relational tools.

Building the Foundation through Communication

When it comes to building a structure of any kind, any guy will tell you first things first. Before the walls and roof and windows and flooring can be assembled or installed, you must . . . *must* . . . have a foundation.

It's that way with our personal relationships too, and when it comes to those relationships, the foundation is communication.

That's right, we're talking about talking.

This means opening up, expressing yourself, expanding your word count, and sharing intimate details—and don't say you don't have intimate details—with the person you love.

We see you guys out there, eyes wide, wincing and backing up as if we were coming at you with a bullwhip. We see you trying to set this book down and pretend you never saw it. Get back here and listen.

Here's a news flash for you: Open sharing has never killed a man. In fact, it has caused illnesses in only a few that we're aware of. So just relax!

There. That's better. Grip the book firmly, and keep reading.

If you're like most men, once you've accepted the fact that you need this relational tool, you'll ask yourself this question: "What's there to talk about?" Women, of course, would laugh at this question. Their question is: "How will we ever find enough time to talk about everything?"

And that brings up this point: When it comes to shopping for relational tools, you must be devoted not only to acquiring them but also to using them often. We're not talking about the type of devotion it requires to keep up with the latest Craftsman tool catalog release. We're talking about a deep devotion—true and steady.

We're talking about the kind of devotion demonstrated by a California man we'll call Hal.

UTTER DEVOTION

Hal loved flying. Hal had tried every legal way possible to get himself airborne. But the military disqualified him from a preflight program because of poor eyesight, and a few years later he flunked out of a private air academy.

Still drawn by the call of the blue sky, Hal bought a house not far from Los Angeles International Airport. His thinking was that maybe, just maybe, he could satisfy his deep devotion to flying by way of osmosis. In other words, the closer he lived to an airport, the more his desire would be satisfied.

Instead, Hal's passion for the air only grew. One day as he sat in his backyard lawn chair, he hit upon an idea. A few days later he hurried to the local Army surplus store and bought some weather balloons—forty-four three-foot-high balloons to be exact. Next he purchased a dozen tanks of helium, then set about perfecting his plan.

A week later Hal called his buddies over to watch his project take flight. He attached the balloons to his comfy lawn chair, filled them with helium, and strapped himself in. He had his buddies hand him a sandwich, a cold beverage, and a pellet gun.

"Okay, guys," he said as he craned his head around and waved at his friends. "Cut 'er loose."

It was supposed to work like this: The guys would cut the ties, and the balloons would float lazily up some twenty or thirty feet over Hal's house, taking him and the lawn chair with them. From that vantage point, Hal would sit back in his chair, eat his sandwich, drink his cold beverage, and pass the time for a few hours. When he was ready to come down, he'd simply use the pellet gun to shoot out a couple balloons, and back to the ground he'd come.

Instead, Hal's buddies cut the chair loose and *zoom!* It shot Hal like a missile straight into the air, passing the thirty-foot mark in fractions of a second and speeding past both the three-hundred- and the three-thousand-foot marks. In fact, it lifted Hal into the air faster than many jumbo jets and finally leveled off at approximately 16,000 feet.

> **GUY FACT**
>
> According to the Department of Commerce, the U.S. leads the world in broken marriages, with 20.7 divorces out of every 1,000 married people.

Now remember, Hal did this because of his love for flying. But dangling some 16,000 feet from earth, suspended by forty-four helium-filled weather balloons, and sitting in a Sears lawn chair, *frightened* doesn't even come close to describing Hal's emotions.

He was scared to death.

Should he shoot out a few balloons and bring himself down? Or would that upset the chair's balance and cause permanent, possibly fatal, damage by spilling him to the ground?

While the options bounced about like pinballs in Hal's mind, he floated perilously into the flight paths of both TWA and Delta Air, and officials from both airlines alerted the Federal Aviation Administration. We wish we could have seen Hal from the vantage point of those pilots. We know enough to say that air traffic was halted immediately.

Meanwhile, things got worse for Hal. The wind currents took him closer to the Pacific Ocean—which is notorious for having no landing areas—and the balloons showed no signs of drifting down to earth.

Figuring he had no choice, Hal dropped his sandwich and cold beverage, picked up the pellet gun, and strategically took out enough weather balloons to bring the chair slowly to the ground, where he made a smooth landing. Once he was down, he was greeted by most of the Los Angeles Police Department, cuffed, and led away in a squad car.

"I didn't mean any harm," Hal explained to the officers. "It's just that I was desperate to fly."

See that? That's the kind of desperation we guys need when it comes to building unforgettable relationships. With that attitude in mind, remember that Jesus owns the relational tool store, and he's running a special. Invest a little time in his storeroom, and he'll give you the tools for free.

Remember earlier when we said that women believe there's much to talk about? The amazing thing is, when you break it down and analyze it, women are right. In fact, there's so much power in communicating that we're going to take this entire chapter to talk about the two relational tools that will best help you talk to the person you love: the open-sharing tool and the patient-listening tool.

Let's get started.

USING THE OPEN-SHARING TOOL

A woman wants meaningful communication and memorable conversations, but instead she gets little more than schoolgirls got decades earlier on the playground. This is because our brains operate so very differently from theirs. And it's this very truth that often makes it difficult for us guys to establish and maintain the relationship we so desperately desire.

There is good news, though. In fact, it's *great* news! When we take hold of the open-sharing tool and learn to use it properly, we can have a relationship like the one in the following story.

Alan had mastered the use of the open-sharing tool. One day the topic of talking came up at a get-together Alan and some other men attended. One man after another complained that he couldn't seem to talk enough for his wife's taste.

"I just don't have it in me," one man said.

That's when Alan spoke up. He told the others how he and his wife, Sue, had agreed that the first fifteen minutes after he got home were for sharing time. On the way into the house after work each day, he reached into his internal toolbox and grabbed his open-sharing tool. Then he'd walk through the door, hug his wife and kids, and set out to the living-room sofa where he and his wife would spend the next fifteen minutes talking with one another. Uninterrupted.

Alan and Sue's kids had been taught that Mom and Dad needed this time together, and they knew better than to bring homework, art projects, or pressing requests to Alan during those fifteen minutes.

"Sue and I face each other, and for the next fifteen minutes we talk," Alan told his male friends.

The men around Alan had blank faces. "About what?" one of them asked.

"We start with her day. She tells me the highs and lows and brings up anything important that came up in the way of phone calls or messages."

"So none of that feelings stuff," a guy in the corner grinned. "Anyone can talk about basic details. But my wife wants feelings."

Alan smiled. "I was getting to that," he said as he turned to the others. "It only takes a few minutes for her to list the details of the day. Then I list the details of mine. After that, the real sharing begins."

"No!" an older man in the back said, and let his jaw drop open. "Right after work?"

Alan chuckled. "Yes. Right after work. I tell her how I'm feeling about me and God, me and the kids, and me and her. How my workday has affected those relationships, and how I feel about what I missed during the day. I ask her questions about her feelings too," he said. "The whole thing almost never takes more than fifteen minutes, and that way she feels like I opened up to her."

Alan went on to say that since Sue was home all day with the kids, he felt it only fair that he make her feel special with those set-apart minutes of open sharing.

"Isn't it hard?" someone asked. "I mean, right after a long day?"

"At first," Alan replied. "But now I look forward to it. And our marriage has never been better."

"In what ways?" There was a glimmer in the eye of the man who asked.

Alan's grin grew. "In every way that matters."

And suddenly every man in the room wanted to get hold of the open-sharing tool and put it to use.

Now that we've looked at an example of using the open-sharing tool, let's talk about how we can use it in our own relationships.

An Open-Sharing Tool User's Guide

Imagine you were married to the woman of your dreams, and both of you lived during the days when the Tower of Babel was built. One day you come home and your wife is speaking Hebrew instead of English.

There you stand—face-to-face, toe-to-toe—each of you bursting with love for the other but with no way to communicate that love.

In a sense, this is a great picture of men and women throughout the ages—with one exception: the language barrier is not sudden or new. Rather, if you're like most people, it has always been in place. If you were living during the Tower of Babel days, you would be desperate to find a way to communicate love, emotions, feelings, and thoughts to the woman you love. And because you didn't speak the same language, you would probably have to be creative.

Today, however, we speak the same language that our wives do. So let's examine some things you can use as you creatively begin using your open-sharing tool.

TOOL TIP

When using the open-sharing tool, always remember that men and women tend to relate and communicate differently. The purpose of this tool is to help you communicate better on her level.

USE YOUR PERSONAL HISTORY

John struggled with talking about his feelings. He found out about the importance of having the open-sharing tool in his relational toolbox, and he latched onto the idea of talking about his personal history as a way of defining his feelings. Things had been difficult for John at work, but he hadn't talked with his fiancée, Carol, about it. One day he decided to experiment with the open-sharing tool.

John waited for a relaxed time when he was alone with Carol. Then he took a deep breath and started this conversation.

"I was really sick as a child . . . did you know that? I almost died."

"No!" Carol gasped, and instantly a deeper sort of love and compassion filled her eyes. "What happened?"

John explained the illness while Carol, with each passing moment, slid closer to him on the sofa, her face filled with shock and sympathy.

Remember, John was looking for a way to tie his personal history with his current situation at work. So after he'd established the past incident, he moved ahead.

"My parents were afraid all the time, never knowing if I'd get sick again or what might happen."

"I can imagine." Carol rested her head on his shoulder for a moment, and then met his eyes once more.

"You know something?"

"What?"

"That's the same way I feel at work these days. Like something could happen any day . . . a layoff or a transfer. It's tough sometimes. Really tough."

Whatever Carol had felt for him before, John believes he is being conservative when he says that the moment he made the analogy, her love for him tripled.

"I could see it in her eyes. It was like we had this bond that wasn't there before."

Not only had John shared something of his past with Carol, he also shared the way he was feeling at work. After that she felt more in touch with John's career and the issues he struggled with on the job. Naturally, this left them emotionally closer than many couples, all because John had been willing to use the open-sharing tool to build his relationship.

Sharing your past experiences is, of course, just one way of using the open-sharing tool.

USE YOUR WORK EXPERIENCE

Ralph was a sales manager who had one employee who routinely made his own travel plans and sales pitches. The employee's behavior went against the grain and threatened to harm the entire department.

At that same time, Ralph's wife routinely withdrew money from their checking account without discussing this with him. In their household, Ralph paid the bills, and he knew how much needed to be paid to whom and by what date. Ralph fought with his wife about this many times, using his problem-solving and fact-giving tools to express his disappointment in her spending habits. But this only served to make his wife angry.

"You don't care about my feelings," she told him time and again.

So Ralph came to us for help, and we suggested the open-sharing tool. Why? Because Ralph's wife needed to understand how Ralph felt about her careless spending. Michael suggested Ralph use the situation at work as a way of explaining his feelings.

Ralph took the advice and his conversation with his wife went something like this:

"Have I told you what's happening at work with one of the salesmen?" Ralph asked his wife.

"No," she replied, and found a seat near him. Her open arms and relaxed features told him she was listening with her heart. She gave him a concerned look. "Tell me."

Ralph talked about his plans for his department at work and how the one employee continued to do things his own way.

> **GUY FACT**
>
> According to *The Guinness Book of Records*, the longest engagement was between Octavio Guillen and Adriana Martinez, who took sixty-seven years to make sure they were right for each other.

"Not much of a team player, honey." His wife leaned closer. "What can you do about it?"

"Well . . . I'm working on it." Ralph took a deep breath. "But that's not the only reason I brought it up."

Then Ralph transitioned the story. "Being married is teamwork too, don't you think?"

"Definitely." His wife nodded, her eyes locked on his.

"Things like parenting or deciding where we'll live. Spending money. You know, anything like that. Those things work best when they're done together—like a team."

His wife nodded, a bit more slowly this time. "I never thought of it that way."

Before long this couple was into a full-blown discussion about money and spending habits and teamwork, a discussion that neither upset nor angered Ralph's wife.

This conversation had an almost miraculous effect on Ralph's marriage. First, his wife felt closer to him, more connected because he'd shared something personal about his job. Second, because her heart was already receptive to that sharing, his wife felt neither defensive nor attacked at Ralph's discussion about their personal finances.

More conversations followed, and Ralph became adept at using the open-sharing tool.

As difficult as it can seem, learning to share your feelings with someone you love is not impossible. And as is true with using any tool, the more you use it, the better you'll be at building something memorable.

MAKE FEELINGS OUT OF FACTS

Since men tend to be more factual, one way of using the open-sharing tool is to combine it with facts. Sometimes this involves a word picture, in which you might take something physical or factual and relate it to how you are feeling.

Here are some examples.

✗ (Showing her an empty box) "Honey, this is how my life feels today."

✗ (In reference to your clean office desk) "Do you know how I cleaned my desk today? I put away everything that was cluttering it, one thing at a time. That's what I want to do with the problems we're dealing with. Take one thing at a time and talk about it. When we're done, our hearts will be clean too."

✗ (Holding up a newspaper) "I could fill a newspaper with all the things that happened today. But let me tell you about one particular story."

✗ (Pointing to the family's marked-up calendar) "We've made time for lots of things this month but not for you and me. Let's find an open date and go out to dinner."

For some of you, identifying how you are feeling or using a feeling word can be challenging. Here is a "feeling words" chart to help you get started:

Feelings

A: accepted, adventurous, aesthetic, afraid, alive, amused, analytical, angry, anxious, apprehensive, articulate, ashamed, atypical, aware

B: bitter, bored

C: capable, caring, centered, charmed, charming, cheerful, cherished, childlike, clever, comfortable, competent, concerned, confident, contemptuous, contented, courageous, creative

D: dejected, delighted, dependable, depressed, despairing, desperate, devastated, disciplined, discouraged, disgusted, doubtful, dynamic

E: effective, embarrassed, empathetic, entertaining, enthusiastic, ethical, exasperated, excited

F: flexible, forgiving, fortunate, frantic, friendly, frightened, frustrated, fulfilled, funny, furious

G: glad, good, great, grounded, guilty

H: happy, helpful, helpless, honest, hopeful, horrified, human, humiliated, hurt

I: insightful, inspiring, integrated, intellectual, intelligent, interesting, irritated

J: joyful

K: kind

L: lonely, lovable, loving, loyal

M: miserable, moral

N: nurturing

O: open, original, overwhelmed

P: peaceful, playful, practical, pragmatic, pressured, productive, provoked

Q: quieted

R: reflective, regretful, relaxed, resentful, resourceful, respected

S: sad, safe, sane, satisfied, scared, secure, sensual, serene, shrewd, special, spiritual, spontaneous, strong

T: thankful, threatened, thrilled, trapped, troubled, trusted, trusting

U: uncomfortable, understood, uneasy, unique, unusual, uptight, useful

V: valuable, versatile

W: warm, wealthy, weird, well-defined, well-loved, whole, wise, wonderful, worn-out, worried, worthwhile

USE WORD PICTURES

Often you intend to be sensitive and intuitive to your wife's wants and needs, but she is unable to grasp your situation. Early on in using the open-sharing tool, you may find it difficult to come up with the words to express yourself. When that happens, try using word pictures.

For example, you explain to your wife that solitude after work is as important to you as gasoline is to a car. Once she grasps this word picture—which for most women will happen instantly—you can easily communicate with her in ways she'll immediately understand.

See if using this type of word picture will help develop your ability to communicate. Remember, these practical helps will enable you to feel successful with your open-sharing tool. And in time and with practice, it'll become a regular part of your relational-building ability.

Remember that most women have a built-in relationship manual. Most of them are born with the relational tools we're talking about, just as most men are born with internal provider/protector tools.

Here is a list of suggestions that could help you become better at using the open-sharing tool:

✗ Choose the time and location of your conversations carefully.
✗ Rather than getting frustrated, explain to the person you love that you will go into greater detail later in the evening, after you've had a chance to unwind.
✗ When the timing is right, encourage the person you love to ask questions that will help you use the open-sharing tool. Yes, questions can be annoying, but often a woman will know exactly which questions to ask in order to trigger an open-sharing moment.
✗ When someone asks multiple questions, pick one and answer it as well as you can, providing the person with facts, feelings, and data.
✗ Have object lessons and factual details ready. These are the starting points for any sharing. Allow them to lead you to the next level of sharing the feelings that go with those object lessons and facts.

Most women feel that every part of a conversation—every thought, every word, every syllable—is highly important and worth sharing. In fact, they're probably bursting at the seams for the chance to share thousands of words with you at day's end. But help her understand that sometimes you don't need to know the details of anything other than what has happened to her, the kids, and the family, or whatever affects any of you directly.[1]

Let's look at some things that will help you become adept at using your open-sharing tool.

Some Final Tips for Using the Open-Sharing Tool
Using the open-sharing tool may seem a little unnatural at first. But we believe that if you understand a few things about this internal tool, you can be a success. Here are the things we want you to remember:

1. Understand that the process takes time. If you are like most guys, you've spent most of your life avoiding deep communication. Remember, it will take time to learn to use the open-sharing tool. Be patient with yourself and with your relationship.

2. Look for times when you might be more aware of your feelings. You probably recognize that some settings and occasions make you more aware of your feelings than others. These times may include a leisurely dinner or meal with your loved one, a long walk, a friend's wedding, a reunion, after an emotional movie or song or book, or after a church service. These are the times to make use of the open-sharing tool.

3. Remember to ask questions that help set the mood for open sharing. Ask simple questions such as, "What are you thinking now?" or "How was your day?" Also ask more thoughtful questions such as, "What are your three favorite things about us?" or "What do you remember about being a kid?" Also, remember to ask specific questions about her family and friends.

4. Commit yourself to answering her questions with more than one word. This gets back to expanding that daily word count. When she asks you specific questions, avoid the one-word answers such as "fine" or "yes." Delve a little deeper. Try to answer the questions in ways that will communicate to her.

5. Incorporate this type of sharing into fun, shared activities. These activities can include dating (even if you've been married for years), dining out, walking, driving with the radio off, and recreational activities such as bowling, hiking, puzzle building (the list can go on and on).

6. Remember that there are good places and times to use your open-sharing tool as well as bad places and times to use it. Good places and times to use the open-sharing tool include—but are not limited to—at the table after dinner, on the sofa when your wife mutes the commercials, on a walk or bike ride, in the car with the radio off, on the front porch when there are no pressing deadlines approaching, and in bed before or after sex (your wife will love hearing your heart at this time).

The bad times to use this particular relational tool include before dinner while you're reading the paper or helping in the kitchen (too much chaos), during a favorite televised sports event or television program (too distracted), on the court while playing an intense tennis match or other sporting event (too distracted), in the car with the radio blaring (too distracted), anywhere in the minutes before an approaching deadline (too focused on the upcoming event), in the midst of sex (highly distracted), and anytime on busy days when you barely have time to talk.

See? Talking about talking wasn't so bad, was it? Now that you have a much better understanding of the open-sharing tool, let's talk about one that—at least on the surface—seems easier.

USING THE PATIENT-LISTENING TOOL

Now hear us on this: Men and women feel differently about the act of listening. According to Deborah Tannen, author of *You Just Don't Understand*, men listen to women less frequently than women listen to men. Why? Because men consider listening a subordinate act.[2]

Yes, you heard us right. If you're like most men, deep inside that testosterone-soaked brain of yours, you consider listening passive or meek, something you can't even begin to relate to. The following chart demonstrates how differently men and women see the act of listening:

HOW MEN FEEL ABOUT LISTENING	HOW WOMEN FEEL ABOUT LISTENING
It's passive.	It's an investment.
It's a sign of meekness.	It's a chance to get to know someone's feelings better.
It means I have nothing to say.	It's polite.
It's a sign of a weak personality.	It's a sign that I'm interested in the other person.
It's time consuming.	It's a privilege.
It traps me into hearing the sometimes unimportant things another person wants to tell me.	It provides me the chance to be heard at a later time.

Did you catch that last part? Women feel that the very act of listening provides them the chance to be listened to. And Tannen agrees with this. Women believe listening should be reciprocal in all their relationships. Simply put, the principle is this: I listen now; you listen later.

So what happens when men don't listen? Feelings get hurt and relationships get torn apart. When we've counseled couples considering divorce, the women often tell us their husbands don't listen. Here are some of the most common statements women make about their husbands' lack of listening:

✗ "He doesn't hear me."
✗ "He doesn't know who I am."
✗ "What I have to say isn't important to him."
✗ "He tunes me out."
✗ "I don't love him anymore because he doesn't take time to listen to me."
✗ "I feel that I'm not important to him."

When women come to one of us at the Smalley Relationship Center and say something like what we've listed above, we tend to go one place for answers—to the guys. We ask the guys, "Why aren't you listening to what this person you love has to say?"

Here are some of the more common responses we get to that question:

✗ "I already know who she is and what she's going to say. I get tired of hearing the same thing over and over."
✗ "I got what she was saying in the first two minutes. I didn't need an hour-long explanation."
✗ "Nothing she's going to tell me is truly news, and there are a dozen other things I need to do besides sit and listen."
✗ "I can listen to more than one thing at a time."
✗ "She's fickle with her feelings. Sometimes I think she talks a long time just to test me."
✗ "It's important to me that we stop fighting, but there are lots of

ways I can show her she's important without having to listen to an hour of useless information or the same story a hundred times over."

Can you see what's missing in each of the statements we receive from men? If you guessed patience, you're right. Patient listening makes a person feel respected, validated, and worthy of love. It fosters trust and value and honor, things we'll talk about more in the next chapter.

We must learn to use the patient-listening tool not only with the women in our lives but also with colleagues and male friends.

The Patient-Listening Tool in Action

Robert had truly mastered the patient-listening tool. One time not long ago, he began to feel a strain in his friendship with Barry, whom he'd known since high school. The change seemed to take place about the same time Robert was promoted to president of a large company. At first it was small things—a flippant comment from Barry about Robert's new house, a snide remark about Robert's social circle. Then Barry and his wife stopped coming by for visits. Eventually Barry stopped calling altogether.

Robert didn't need to be the brightest bulb on the Christmas tree to realize Barry was angry at him about something. Robert's wife was also feeling the strain in the relationship. Barry's wife was giving her the cold shoulder at church and virtually refusing to contact her the way she once had.

"They aren't our friends anymore," Robert's wife declared one day. "Better to just let them go."

But Robert had other ideas. He contacted his friend and suggested in a calm voice that they get together and talk. But Barry seemed reluctant. "You don't understand what I'm seeing," Barry said. "You've changed, Robert. You don't have time for people like me."

Barry's hurt tone of voice and his accusation took Robert by surprise. At that moment, Robert could easily have gotten defensive, shouted at his friend, told him he was wrong, and hung up the phone. In fact, it could've been the end of their friendship right there.

Instead, Robert listened patiently until Barry was finished. Then he simply said, "Where would you like to meet, Barry?"

They decided on Barry's house—mostly because Robert wanted his friend to feel comfortable in his own setting. "If he has legitimate concerns, I want to hear them," he told his wife before he left. "Pray that I'll be a good listener."

TOOL TIP

Patient listening means just that.
You must learn to really hear what the other person is saying.

On the way to Barry's house, Robert pulled his well-used patient-listening tool from his internal toolbox. By the time the discussion with his friend started, Robert was ready. It started with his posture. Robert took a chair near Barry's and sat at the edge of the seat, bent partially over, his arms resting on his knees. Next, the patient-listening tool helped Robert make constant, kind eye contact with his friend.

Robert determined that he would use the patient-listening tool until Barry had nothing left to say. While Barry talked, Robert nodded and made little sounds of agreement or understanding.

"It feels like you've become some sort of big shot, like you don't have time for me," Barry said, then crossed his arms, his eyebrows knit together.

"Okay, tell me why." Robert kept his voice gentle.

"Because you go to dinner parties with people who are millionaires."

"Why does that bother you, Barry?"

And so it went. By the end of the evening, Barry had talked through all his concerns and insecurities and had come to a simple realization, one that wasn't easy to admit.

"Maybe I was reading more into it than I should have." Barry gave Robert a sheepish grin. "But thanks for letting me vent."

Letting a person you care about vent is exactly what the patient-listening tool is all about. Whether it's a frustrated friend or a frazzled wife, sometimes we build the best relationships by learning to listen—*just listen.*

Tips for Using the Patient-Listening Tool

Now we want to give you some practical pointers for using your patient-listening tool. These are the things we've learned in our own relationships and through our counseling sessions.

1. Make and keep eye contact. Few things assure your loved one that you are listening closely more than making eye contact. Without making it seem like you are staring through her, lock your eyes on hers and listen to what she has to say—all of what she has to say.

2. Cease all other activity. When your loved one wants to talk to you—when she has something very important to talk to you about and needs your undivided attention—make sure you can do that in an atmosphere free of other activity. Going for a walk is a great setting for this kind of listening, but playing tennis or engaging in other physical activities is not.

3. Let your loved one know you are being attentive. In addition to keeping eye contact, let her know that you are listening closely and attentively by acknowledging what she's saying through head nods and other signs of attentiveness.

4. Speak occasional words of agreement or understanding. While you listen to your loved one, it is good to interject words that communicate that you understand how that person feels. Simple statements such as, "I can see how you would feel that way," or "I would feel the same way myself" can do much to communicate that you are patiently listening.

5. Ignore all interruptions. Sometimes a man and his loved one need to get to a place where there is no chance they will be interrupted so they can just talk. When you take the time to patiently listen to your loved one, try to do it where you won't be interrupted.

Okay, now that you have an idea of what patient listening is and the importance of it in a relationship, let's see what the buyer's guide says about becoming an expert at using this tool. Remember, a little listening goes a long way.

Becoming an Expert with the Patient-Listening Tool
As we've already mentioned, we've surveyed thousands of women in preparing to write this book. One of the questions we asked was this: How can a man become an expert at patient listening?

Here are some of their answers:

✗ "Solve problems with me, not for me."
✗ "Just listen. Give me a chance to voice my inner thoughts and feelings."
✗ "Listen without offering unsolicited advice or blame."
✗ "Teach me your problem-solving skills."
✗ "If you don't understand what I'm saying, ask me questions."
✗ "Offer feedback that says you understand what I'm telling you."
✗ "Be compassionate as you listen."
✗ "Resist laughing or mocking me in what I have to say."
✗ "Offer me advice with humility."
✗ "Use facial expressions and body language so that I know you're really hearing me."

Do you hear the feelings behind these statements? Can you see how our impatience hurts the ones we love? Realizing this can motivate us to practice the patient-listening tool.

In the next chapter we'll take a somewhat quicker look at the other relational tools. That is not because they are less important than the two we've covered in this chapter. But as any guy who knows about building will tell you, once a strong foundation is laid, the rest practically takes care of itself.

Building the Relationship through Behavior

One summer Randy, a grade-school teacher, had to move his family across town into a bigger house. In order to do the job, he solicited the services of a U-Haul van and a friend named Rob.

Early one Saturday morning Randy and Rob headed down to the U-Haul lot, where Randy filled out the paperwork.

"One day or two?" the guy behind the counter asked.

Randy stopped writing, his pen suspended in air. "What's the difference in price?"

The guy leveled his gaze at Randy. "A hundred bucks if it's back by eight o'clock. Two hundred if it's back tomorrow by eight."

Today Randy admits that the U-Haul guy was probably not trying to issue a challenge. But in that moment, the two friends exchanged a glance that said they'd just entered into a competition.

The goal: Get the truck back by eight o'clock.

The prize: one hundred dollars!

"Go ahead . . . " Randy lowered his chin, his tone as close to Clint Eastwood's as it would ever get. "Make it one day."

With that, Randy and Rob got to work. They loaded and unloaded until dusk, and at just after six o'clock, they finally pulled up to Randy's new house with the last of his family's belongings.

"This is it," Randy said as he backed up. "We're gonna beat the clock."

Both men's wives and their children stood on the lawn watching Randy quickly back the truck in. But for whatever reason—Randy says he was perhaps in too big a hurry—he backed that U-Haul truck right into the garage wall.

Randy heard a sickening thud of the truck connecting with the wall and a crash, as inside the U-Haul three free-standing lamps fell across boxes of dishes. He felt the distinct sensation of something giving.

GUY FACT

In 1892 the minimum age for marriage of Italian girls was raised by law to twelve years.

"Oh, no!" Randy shouted. And he meant it.

He climbed out of the truck and saw that he'd moved the garage wall some two feet closer to the house.

"You're in deep trouble, friend," Rob offered.

Randy hopped back into the truck and pulled it forward a few feet. He got back out; then he and Rob surveyed the damage. That's when they saw the worst part: Randy had caused a major buckle in the bumper of the U-Haul.

About that time, the wives and children recovered from their shock enough to move in and comment on the incident. But Randy and Rob heard none of it. They merely looked at each other and knew in the deepest places of their hearts that they were thinking the same thing: *This is going to make us late.*

Since the truck was full of mainly small and light items, Randy delegated the job of unloading to the wives and children.

"We need to fix the bumper," Randy said, his eyes glazed over.

"I've got tools," Rob said. It wasn't that Randy didn't have tools; it's just that they were packed away.

Without another word Randy and Rob hopped in Rob's car, darted across town, then returned with Rob's tools. One of the tools Rob thought to grab from his garage was—we're completely serious here—his blowtorch.

The men set to work at seven o'clock, knowing fully that they had just one hour to fix the truck and get it back by eight. Randy wanted to fix the bumper with the hammer, but Rob was certain the blowtorch was the answer. Unable to decide which would be more effective, the men took turns. For the next forty-five minutes, they tried melting the bumper, hammering the bumper, and prying the bumper straight. But nothing worked even a little.

Finally, and sadly, the men admitted defeat. Rob patted Randy on the back. "It's okay," he said. "We can still get it back on time."

They took the U-Haul back and reported the damage. The result: One-day's charge for the use of the truck and $150 in bumper repair costs.

The thing was, Randy and Rob never fought with one another about this. In the course of a day they had tackled an enormous project—moving—and done the entire thing side-by-side without complaining. Not only that, but they'd done it operating under the self-imposed rules of competition—finish by eight or else. And when things went wrong, neither of them pointed a finger or shouted at the other.

They merely stayed united and worked together to face the consequences of their situation.

Now imagine for a moment that this one-day U-Haul adventure represented a relationship. What tools allowed Randy and Rob to work so well together? Here's what we think:

1. The win-win tool. Randy wanted to use the hammer, and Rob, the blowtorch, but in light of the bigger task at hand, they compromised and took turns using both tools, thereby avoiding an argument.

2. Selfless-honor tool. Rob honored Randy by never pointing a finger or accusing him. Once the damage was done, both men were committed to moving forward with the situation.

3. Tender-touch tool. Rob gave Randy a pat on the back as a way of commiserating with him.

4. Time-and-energy tool. Rob agreed to spend his Saturday helping Randy move.

Now, we'd be willing to bet neither Randy nor Rob ever imagined for a minute that their daylong adventure with the U-Haul truck could illustrate how relational tools can affect our behavior. But the truth is, it works.

These four tools can shape and change our behavior so we can get along not just with our buddies on moving day but also with our families, coworkers, and other friends.

Let's take a look at these four relational tools, starting with the win-win tool.

THE WIN-WIN TOOL

You remember the win-win tool, the one that helps us guys give in to our loved ones' desires once in a while, the one that helps us demonstrate how much we honor the way they think and feel.

Here is an example of the win-win tool in action.

A couple we know used to argue every spring over where they'd spend their summer vacations. Bill wanted to travel the country, visit exciting places, and learn foreign languages. But Cheryl wanted a week with her family in Ohio, complete with backyard barbecues and reunion gatherings. Bill's family was spread out across the country and rarely visited each other. But Cheryl's family was very closely knit—a little too closely knit in Bill's opinion.

Bill first learned to use his win-win tool early in their marriage when he agreed that Cheryl's type of vacation was just as important and valid as his. He worked out a compromise by taking two vacation weeks each summer—one for an adventure trip with his family and one to rekindle ties with Cheryl's family in Ohio.

But last summer Bill's use of the win-win tool improved to the expert level. It started because Cheryl had a convention she needed to attend for work. And wouldn't you know, the convention was in Dayton, Ohio, just an hour from Cheryl's family! The problem was it took place the week before Cheryl's parents' family reunion.

"I know," Cheryl said one day that spring. "Let's take a few days and drive to Ohio. You can spend the first week visiting with my family while I attend the convention. And the second week we'll spend there together."

This made Bill think that he'd spend *both* his vacation weeks with Cheryl's family; Cheryl saw it as two separate vacations—one with her and one without her.

"You know how I love driving trips, Bill. Please!" Cheryl lowered her chin and batted her eyelashes.

Bill could only blink in return. Was she kidding? Drive from North Carolina to Dayton, Ohio, drop Cheryl off at her convention, turn around and head an hour in the opposite direction to Cheryl's parents' house? Then spend a week there with the kids and virtually nothing to do? Drive back to Dayton to pick up Cheryl, then back to her parents' house for another week of family get-togethers?

> ## GUY FACT
> The average duration of nuptial ceremony at Las Vegas's "Little White Chapel," home of the world's only drive-through wedding window, is 7 minutes.

Cheryl's parents' house was only half the size of Bill and Cheryl's house, so the two of them would sleep on a pull-out sofa bed while the kids would camp on the floor around them. For two weeks.

Only one thing came to Bill's mind: "Are you serious?" he asked her.

Cheryl looked at him for a moment. "Of course I'm serious. Think of how much fun we'll have on the drive up."

"We have four kids, Cheryl. That isn't exactly fun on a two-day road trip, especially living out of a suitcase."

Cheryl's smile faded, and Bill could sense her frustration the way a smoke alarm senses a fully involved house fire. Suddenly he knew with the sort of instinct that comes after using the relational tools for some time that this was the moment to bring out the win-win tool. He began to reason with himself. This was the first time Cheryl had ever made such a request, and besides, a road trip could be fun, couldn't it?

He walked up to Cheryl, placed his hands on her shoulders, and looked her straight in the eyes. "Honey, if it's what you want to do, then fine," he said. "Let's go ahead and do it."

Okay, now we know a lot of you guys are about to rip this page out, ready to shout to whoever will listen, "Now wait a minute! That isn't fair!" And guess what? You're right, it wasn't fair. Bill had some very valid concerns about their vacation plans. But he'd learned long ago that the win-win tool goes a long way toward building happier relationships. So he weighed the gains and losses on this one and decided to let Cheryl have her way.

You won't believe what wound up happening.

Cheryl—who until the moment Bill gave in had been ready to fight about the matter—stepped back, thanked Bill, and went silent. The next morning she did something Bill will remember as long as he lives. She walked downstairs, met him at the kitchen table, and said, "Bill, maybe you're right."

GUY FACT

A couple living together for two years in Russia is considered married. This is called a citizen marriage.

"About what?"

"About the vacation."

Bill drew a blank. "Okay."

"What I mean is, I thought about it and it doesn't really make sense. If we do it my way, you and the kids will spend two weeks at my parents' house." She shook her head as though she were still only now understanding the bigger picture. "That doesn't sound like a great vacation to me."

Bill worked hard to keep from smiling. "Okay."

"So what I'm saying is, I think we can keep our usual plans. Even though the convention's in Ohio, I'll fly in, and then a week later you and the kids can meet me for our family vacation." She grinned as though she'd just figured it out. "That way we can save your other week of vacation for something you'd like to do."

And that, friends, is what happens when you skillfully use the win-win tool. Bill made his desires secondary to Cheryl's, showing her that he valued her and her needs.

Achieving a win-win situation means one thing—give and take. In order to build a successful relationship, you must take hold of the truth that a relationship can be successful only if there is give and take. According to author Deborah Tannen, men and women struggle with these two forces every time they talk. The woman is trying to connect through words and feelings, and the man is trying to wield his take-charge tool so as not to feel controlled or inferior.

TOOL TIP

Spend one hour each week in an activity that is meaningful to someone you love.

The Win-Win Tool: Its Uses and Benefits

The win-win tool can be helpful in dealing with a variety of issues within your relationship. Those issues include handling money, how to spend a Friday or Saturday night, how to decorate the house, where to go on vacation, what kinds of hobbies or activities the two of you can share, and—this is a huge one—how to raise children.

Again, we turned to our surveys for ways women tell us we men can be better at using the win-win tool. Here are a few of the things they had to say:

✗ "Meet me in the middle."

✗ "Understand my needs and allow my opinions to count for part of the decision-making process in our relationship."

✗ "Assert your opinion in a loving, equal way."

✗ "Talk over decisions that must be made."

✗ "Add softness to your tone when we are making decisions together."

✗ "Remember that I am not the enemy."
✗ "Back down once in a while."
✗ "Realize that my heart is fragile."
✗ "Use kind words."
✗ "Apologize when you're wrong."

Good advice. Hearing these responses and acting on them will bring you that much closer to a satisfying relationship. And because your loved one sees you making your relationship a priority, she will be more likely to trust you. In addition, once your loved one sees you "bending" more often, she will be more likely to let you have your way more often. You will also learn the art of working together with someone you love.

USING THE SELFLESS-HONOR TOOL

When we can make use of the selfless-honor tool, it benefits just about any kind of relationship. That is especially true of our relationship with our wives. This relational tool helps us think of her first, and it helps us verbalize our love.

Troy gives us an amazing example of the use of the selfless-honor tool. He constantly found ways to compliment his wife and children, making a point to notice ways that they were special or unique. But Troy's best example of using this particular relational tool took place one summer.

Troy is a middle-school science teacher, so usually he has the summers off. In the past this has given Troy the chance to take a college course or work a part-time job in the university science lab near his Los Angeles home. But last summer Troy's wife, Sheila, had the chance to enter a screenwriting competition. There was one problem. The children were two, three, and five that year and constantly underfoot. Sheila was a stay-at-home mom, and the family couldn't afford day care while Sheila took time to write her screenplay.

"It would never work out," she told Troy one day after dinner. "The kids need me."

Now hear us on this: The selfless-honor tool is a multipurpose tool, sort of the Swiss Army knife of relational tools. Troy took hold of it and first honored his wife by saying, "Sheila, you're a wonderful writer. Enter the contest, honey, because you'll probably write the best screenplay of all." He gave her a crooked smile. "That way you can sign a million-dollar contract, and I'll live a life of leisure." His smile faded some. "Seriously, Sheila, if this is important to you, we have to make it work."

There is simply no way to calculate the worth of a comment like this in building relationships with the people you love. Troy was aware that his wife loved to write. He had taken the time to read her work, and therefore he was able to make this unforgettable comment. Still, Sheila didn't see a way around their obstacles.

> **GUY FACT**
>
> The observatory of New York City's Empire State Building is considered by many to be the most romantic place to be married.

"But we can't afford help," she countered. "And you've got your job at the university."

The thing was, Troy's summer position wasn't a paid one. It was merely something he enjoyed, something that helped keep his mind sharp for his work of teaching science to young teenagers. Still wielding the selfless-honor tool, Troy took a deep breath and plunged ahead. "I could stay home this summer. You know, be Mr. Mom while you write. How would that be?"

Sheila's face lit up like the Fourth of July. "Are you serious?"

"Completely." Troy didn't say this with a twitch in his lip or a grimace on his face. He was good enough with the selfless-honor tool that he was simply willing to forego something he enjoyed in order to value the woman he loved.

The early summer that year in Troy and Sheila's home was something out of a family comedy. Burned oatmeal, missing socks, and dirty laundry were the benchmarks of their existence. But Troy was a quick learner. By summer's end he was able to wash the white load without accidentally letting a single red object into the washing machine.

Meanwhile, the family benefited in a myriad of ways. Troy made lifelong memories through the time spent with his children, and he made his wife feel cherished and worthwhile in her talents. He also gave Sheila the chance to write a screenplay that won third place in the contest.

No, Sheila wasn't offered a million-dollar writing contract. But this couple's marriage was made forever stronger simply because Troy was willing and able to use the selfless-honor tool.

How We Use the Selfless-Honor Tool and What We Get from It
No marriage—or any other close relationship, for that matter—will lack opportunities to use the selfless-honor tool. You can use it when your loved one is tired or sick or when she is discouraged. You can use it simply to give your loved one a pleasant surprise.

The women we surveyed gave us these specific ways we can use the selfless-honor tool:

✗ "Talk to me and appreciate the things in my heart."
✗ "Let me know when I do something right."
✗ "Trust me to make good choices that affect us both."
✗ "Compliment me, and know that it will draw me closer to you."
✗ "Appreciate specific things about me."
✗ "See me as your friend and ally."
✗ "Build me up and realize that in doing so, you build us up."
✗ "Look at me in the best possible light and let me know that's how you see me."
✗ "Know that by saying kind things to me, you are satisfying me in a thousand ways."
✗ "Let me know that I'm important to you and that my feelings are important to you."

Which of these responses might reflect your wife's feelings? How can you meet that need through selfless honor?

One quick word of warning: Many affairs and illicit relationships start because men give well-meaning praise to women. Keep your praise focused on your wife and daughters. Find ways to see them as winners, treasures whom God has put in your life.

As you learn to make better use of the selfless-honor tool, your loved one will feel confident and secure, and she will feel a closer connection to you. In addition, you will see her as valuable and will begin to appreciate specific qualities about her.

WARNING:
Be careful whom you compliment and affirm.

TAKING HOLD OF TENDER TOUCH

The tender-touch tool is using touch—tender touch—to communicate your love. This kind of touch can include hugs, embraces, and gentle touches.

Blake became a master at the use of the tender-touch tool. A bunch of men were gathered at Blake's home, talking about their families. Most of the men had teenage daughters, and the ones who did were complaining about one aspect or another of their kids' behavior.

"It's the loud cars I can't stand," said one of the men as he shook his head and leaned back. "The guys that come by the house have no respect for anyone else in the neighborhood."

Another man nodded. "I get that all the time. But for me it's my daughter's behavior that turns my face red."

Blake sat near the center of the room, listening intently.

The man with the misbehaving daughter continued: "It started with hand-holding and moved on to kissing. Now she and this . . . this guy she's seeing stand out on the porch and have all-out make-out sessions." He bit his lip and gave a light huff. "If she does that in public, I don't have to ask what's happening behind closed doors. I know. I was a teenager once too."

That was all Blake could handle hearing. At the first break in the conversation, he sat up a bit straighter and looked around the room. "How many of you actually hug your daughters?"

The room fell quiet.

Finally one brave man near the back of the room spoke up. "I used to hug her, when she was little."

"Sure," the first man said. "Me too. But then they get older and, well, you know. They don't want to hug their dads."

Blake gave them a sad smile. "But the truth is, that's when they need us most of all." Then he launched into a story about his use of the tender-touch tool when it came to his daughter, Kelsey.

"Kelsey used to climb up on my lap and cuddle with me all the time." Blake smiled, letting himself remember those days for just a moment. "Then, I don't know, sometime after she hit the fifth grade, I'd pat my knee and smile. And she'd tilt her head and say, 'Daaaad. I'm too old for that.' "

The men around the room nodded. "It was just like that for me," one of them said in a quiet voice.

"At first I figured our cuddling days were over," Blake said. "But then I started reading about teenage girls and how they seek physical love from other places if they're not getting hugs from their fathers." Blake's eyes were intense now, his voice strong. "There was no way I was going to let that happen to Kelsey."

"So what'd you do?" asked the man whose daughter liked making out on the porch.

"I found other ways to erase the gap of time."

For the next ten minutes Blake explained what he did to save his relationship with Kelsey. He would play soccer with her in the front yard, sometimes playfully tackling her to the ground.

"Both of us would be going for the ball and next thing we knew, we'd be having a tickling contest or chasing each other in circles until we fell in a heap laughing." He looked around the room. "Before I knew it, she was back to her old self. She'd find me watching TV and she'd plop herself down on my knee and hug me. 'Love you, Daddy,' she'd say. Then she'd be on her way."

One of the men scratched his head. "So you hug her every day, is that it?"

"Lots of times every day. That's just how we are now. And I'll tell you something else." His eyes sparkled with the victory he was about to share. "She's a junior in high school, and she's never had a serious boyfriend. Lots of friends, of course, but no one she wants to make out with on the front porch."

So there you have it. The perfect example of how the tender-touch tool can be used to build a life-changing father-daughter relationship. Of course, it goes a long way with our sons and brothers, fathers and uncles. And especially with our wives. A ten-minute back rub may seem like no big deal to you. But to your wife, it may be the quickest way to show her you love her.

Tender Touch: When to Use It and What It Does

We guys can use the tender-touch tool in a variety of circumstances and in a variety of ways. It can be a source of comfort for our loved ones, and it can validate their emotions. We can use it when a loved one is not feeling well physically or emotionally, or when she is discouraged. We can use it to help her relax or to simply show her support.

In our surveys, women gave us dozens of ways we guys can use the tender-touch tool. Here are a few of them:

✗ "Hug me after a long day."
✗ "Put your arm around me when I'm crying."
✗ "Hold my hand in public."
✗ "Rub my hands when we're watching television."
✗ "Play with my hair."
✗ "Rub my back—not my bottom—when I'm working in the kitchen."
✗ "Kiss me like you used to when we first started dating."

✗ "Whisper in my ear."

✗ "Lay my head on your shoulder when we're sitting together."

✗ "Hold me after we make love."

We encourage you to take two of these suggestions and put them into practice during the next week. If you do, your wife will feel closer to you and more connected with you. She will also feel more valued. As is the case with the other relational tools, when you use the tender-touch tool, your loved ones will have a deeper sense of trust for you.

SPENDING TIME AND ENERGY

Using the time-and-energy tool simply means that you intentionally spend time and energy on your loved one. That can mean a lot of things and take on a lot of different looks.

Here is how this relational tool looks in the hands of a man with a son who is "wired" differently from his other children.

A friend of ours witnessed her husband, Don, take part in the perfect demonstration of the time-and-energy tool. Don is the father of six children, five of them boys. Nearly every child in the family shares Don's love of sports. With those kids, it's easy for Don to find shared activities together. Most of them are competitive, and that's okay. The sports-driven children love competition. But Don's oldest son, Tyler, is more artistic. He enjoys singing and playing the piano and acting. In many families, a father would be tempted to force a boy like Tyler into a footrace or a one-on-one competition on the basketball court.

Not Don.

One weekend night not long ago, after the dinner dishes were done, the children retired to the TV room to play a card game. All except Tyler, who moved into the living room, slipped in a Broadway CD and began singing songs from long-ago musicals. Don had a choice. He'd spent much of the day playing basketball, soccer, and swimming with his more sports-oriented children. He could play cards with them in the TV room, slip upstairs to read a magazine article and rest, or he could mosey into the living room and play with Tyler.

Using his best imitation Michael Crawford voice, Don became the Phantom of the Opera, whirling around the living room singing songs. Tyler, meanwhile, caught the fire and began improvising the role of a different character from the same play. They laughed and played and before long they were making up silly lines.

"Let's do the moon walk, Dad!" Tyler jumped up and began moving his feet like Michael Jackson. "Come on, you can do it!"

Another choice, but it was easy for Don because he had a firm grasp on his time-and-energy tool. He stood up and held his hands out to his sides like a ballerina. Then with a goofy look on his face, he tried the moon walk. The results were so hilarious, Tyler fell to the floor laughing. Why? Because it wasn't a competition. It was simply a father and son sharing time together in a way that built a bridge between them. A bridge that will help them stay close throughout Tyler's growing-up years and into his adulthood.

The shared dramatics that night went on for an hour, and not once did Don look at the clock. How much time had passed didn't matter. He had no limits on Tyler that evening because he was working on their relationship. The beautiful thing about Don is he does it without thinking. And that's what'll happen with you once you've had some practice with the time-and-energy tool.

How to Spend Your Time and Energy
As we prepared to write this book, we soon realized that if we listed every way we guys can use the time-and-energy tool in our relationships, we'd run out of space to cover the other tools. So we narrowed it down a bit.

A few of the many ways we can use the time-and-energy tool are these: taking a walk after work, getting away for a weekend, going somewhere special for a summer vacation, calling each other during breaks at work, doing a puzzle together on a rainy afternoon, playing tennis or golf on a sunny morning, going grocery shopping together, and planning the week's events together.

Trust us, this list can go on and on. Suffice it to say that you should have no trouble finding ways to use the time-and-energy tool. Here are some of the specific ways women told us we guys can use this relational tool:

✗ "Help me around the house."
✗ "Spend your time with me and not your buddies."
✗ "Tell me jokes and make me laugh."
✗ "Defend me if someone else attacks me in a group setting."
✗ "Be around to make memories with me."
✗ "Play games with me."
✗ "Take a walk with me."
✗ "Take time in our lovemaking."
✗ "Involve me in your sports."
✗ "Read aloud with me."

Once again, these are very good suggestions. Pick two to practice with the people you love.

TOOL TIP

Spend one hour each week in an activity that is meaningful to someone you love.

You can never—and we repeat, never—go wrong using the time-and-energy tool in your relationships. In addition to making your loved ones feel closer to you, you will make them feel more valued simply because they'll know you enjoy their company. You will also get to know them better and make beautiful memories with them.

Since many guys tell us they need help in their relationship with their wives, we've listed some effective ways to spend some romantic time together. But first, a list of actions to avoid.

ROMANCE BREAKERS

✗ Complain about spending time with her.

✗ High-five her when she needs a hug.

✗ Challenge her to a game of one-on-one when she wants a dinner date.

✗ Yawn and complain of being tired.

✗ Listen to her only during commercial breaks.

✗ Read the newspaper while she's talking about her day.

✗ Say "No, not really" when she asks if you want to talk.

✗ Say "Nothing" when she asks what's on your mind.

✗ Forget to notice her new haircut.

✗ Complain about the smell when she has lit candles around the room.

✗ When you sit down to a dinner she's made, suggest that you would rather have ordered pizza.

ROMANCE BUILDERS

✗ Suggest that the two of you should spend more time together on fun dates.

✗ Hold her hand often.

✗ Arrange a surprise dinner date at her favorite restaurant.

✗ Act alert and interested in who she is and what she's feeling.

✗ Turn off the television and give her your full attention.

✗ Put away the newspaper, and make eye contact with her while she's talking.

✗ Share a favorite memory from your childhood when she wants to talk.

✗ Share something specific about your day.

✗ Look for ways to compliment her.

✗ Thank her when she goes to the trouble of creating ambience and atmosphere for you.

Okay, so we've picked up six basic relational tools, and we've spent some time learning how to use them to build successful relationships. We've even looked at the benefits of using them—benefits for our loved ones, for ourselves, and for the relationships.

"That's fine, guys," you say. "But I'm not trying to *build* a relationship. I'm trying to *fix* one. What about me? What tools do I need?"

Good question.

The answers are just ahead in the next chapter.

Forgiveness: The Tool for Repairing Any Relationship

Up to this point we've talked about the relational tools we can use to build healthy, happy relationships. While we can use most of those relational tools to repair a damaged or hurting relationship, their primary purpose is to *build.*

We're going to finish this book by talking about the one relational tool whose purpose is to repair what is damaged, and that's the forgiveness tool. This is the tool each and every one of us needs in order to repair—often *daily* repair—the relationships that matter most to us. Forgiveness is absolutely essential to keeping a relationship healthy and growing.

Gary will share a story that illustrates forgiveness in action as well as its role in repairing and strengthening a relationship.[1]

BETRAYED BY A BROTHER

I thought going into business with my best friend was a dream come true. Dale owned a small company that sold health-food products, and he was very good at what he did. A charismatic leader, he was totally committed to his business.

The year after I joined him in 1968, we doubled the size of the company. The next year we doubled it again. Soon Dale was speaking to audiences all over the country, and I was opening and managing regional offices in ten cities. We were a company on the move.

To say that Dale and I were close is an understatement. We not only worked and traveled together, but we also shared everything: our possessions, our personal dreams, and our vision for the company. We were like brothers. We could talk about anything. I remember nights when we would sit up late into the night dreaming big dreams, praying together, inspiring and encouraging each other. Dale was also my spiritual confidant. I trusted him with my deepest thoughts and confessions.

But nine years into our close friendship, things began to change. The business had expanded to the point that our head office burst with more than a hundred employees. The decisions Dale and I once made while fishing together were made in boardrooms with managers who held MBAs and lots of ideas that seemed to clash with the warm family atmosphere that once marked the company. Conflict became more common, and distrust grew.

While I was distressed to see the company changing, I was even more devastated when Dale started to shut me out. Suddenly I had to knock before entering his office. I was told I was not needed at key decision-making meetings. It soon became clear that he no longer valued my input or our relationship.

When I learned that a few of the managers were involved in some unethical business practices, I went to Dale to express my uneasiness. He dismissed me—and my concerns. I was stunned.

For days after that meeting, I fell into a debilitating depression that sapped my energy. I felt rejected.

And betrayed.

The conflict with Dale cost me a treasured friendship and eventually my job. Our relationship needed lots of repair.

I carried around a great deal of anger toward Dale. And it was beginning to destroy me. What would I do with all of that hurt and resentment? How would I get beyond my devastation?[2]

I knew I needed to forgive Dale, so I forgave him in my heart.

I wish I could tell you that the hurt, pain, and anger melted away. But they didn't.

I finally recognized that I needed God's help, that I couldn't forgive Dale on my own. I longed for freedom and prayed every day to be released from my resentment.

It took two years. I read an article about a situation similar to mine. It was as if God handed me the article, and through it he opened my eyes about why Dale had hurt me. I began to understand my friend, and I could finally see his broken heart and hurts. Gradually his actions and attitude toward me didn't feel personal anymore. I actually felt sorrow for him. I got on my knees for three hours and prayed for him, listing all of the hurts I felt and forgiving him for them one at a time.

God was faithful. Three weeks later, I was free, and my heart was healing. I knew that the forgiveness was complete when I began to feel love for Dale again.

Today Dale and I enjoy a restored relationship, and forgiveness was a major tool in the process.

WHY IS FORGIVENESS SO IMPORTANT?

We live in a fallen world, and each of us is going to make mistakes that affect not only ourselves but also the people around us—particularly those who are most important to us. For that reason we need to be ready and able to ask for and receive forgiveness.

Forgiveness is also important because it has a very positive impact on marital satisfaction. At the Smalley Relationship Center, our director of research, Dr. Peter Larson, did a study that showed that a person's ability to forgive accounted for one-third of the satisfaction within his or her marriage. So if you want to have a satisfying marriage, one of the best things you can do is to forgive your wife and seek out forgiveness when you hurt her or any of your loved ones.

God knows that we need to forgive and to ask forgiveness in order to restore and repair our relationships. Here are the reasons we believe forgiveness is so important.

We Are Made in God's Image

The Bible tells us in the book of Genesis that God made us in his own image. We believe that being made in his image carries with it a tremendous amount of honor and responsibility—honor in knowing our value because of our likeness to the Creator, and responsibility because it is God's nature to forgive.

The apostle John talked about God's forgiving nature in his first epistle: "If we confess our sins, he is faithful and just and will forgive us our sins and purify us from all unrighteousness" (1 John 1:9). Obviously, forgiveness is vitally important to those of us who strive to be more Christlike in everything we do. After all, if God's nature did not consist of forgiveness, where would we be? God knows the awesome power of forgiveness, and he graciously uses it to cleanse us of all our sins.

Since part of God's nature is to forgive, then shouldn't we, as those created in his image, also have it in our nature to forgive? John makes that point: "Whoever loves his brother lives in the light, and there is nothing in him to make him stumble. But whoever hates his brother [i.e. does not forgive or reconcile] is in the darkness and walks around in the darkness; he does not know where he is going, because the darkness has blinded him" (1 John 2:10-11).

When we refuse to follow in God's likeness and will, when we don't learn to forgive as he forgives, we find only pain and suffering.

Forgiveness Is One Way We Can Love As God Loves

The French writer and moralist François duc de La Rochefoucauld wrote in the 1600s, "We pardon to the extent that we love." That's a great description of God's love, isn't it?

When we decide to forgive someone for harming us, we decide to love that person the way God loves us—unconditionally. On the other hand, if we choose not to forgive, we put up limits and boundaries on our love for other people, including those who are closest to us.

Forgiveness is hard work. It's not easy to love people when they have offended or hurt or harmed us. But it's God's way. He gives us his grace to love people in spite of what they have done to us.

Forgiveness Frees the Soul

Forgiveness allows us to break the bonds of anger, rage, hatred, and vengeance. We know that these emotions prevent us from maturing into what God intends us to be. They are toxins to the soul. And forgiveness is the cleanser. Much of the work in therapy today focuses on the issue of forgiveness.

Gary had a choice to make when Dale betrayed him. He could have refused to forgive him for his actions, or he could forgive him and allow the work of Christ to heal them both. Through God's grace Gary chose the path of forgiveness, and their friendship has survived.

If we refuse to forgive others for their mistakes—past mistakes or ones they make in their relationship with us—we allow our relationships to remain broken. Unforgiveness will destroy the relationship with your loved one, but even more devastating is the fact that it will hinder all of that person's future relationships, especially his or her relationship with God. Consider this story.

Daniel was a teenage drug user and in terrible trouble. With nowhere to turn, he moved from shelter to shelter, carrying with him his addiction—and an intense, hidden anger against his father.

"You'll never amount to anything!" Daniel's father used to shout at him when he faltered. "You're worthless!"

But Daniel was immune to it—or so he said to himself and others. "It doesn't bother me," he told his friends.

But the problems with drugs only grew worse.

Daniel didn't understand why he continually fell on what felt like bad luck. "Why is this happening to me?" he would ask. And the anger and unforgiveness continued to grow.

Seventeen years later—lying half awake on a hospital bed after several hours of surgery to repair his liver, which had been devastated by alcohol abuse—Daniel learned how important forgiveness really is. His own son, a born-again Christian, approached his bedside and gently laid his hand on Daniel's sweaty forehead.

"I forgive you," was all his son said.

Suddenly Daniel understood why he suffered for so many years.

He had never forgiven his father for verbally abusing him. In the process, he had harmed *his* son. But those three simple words—I forgive you—released Daniel from a lifetime of pain and inspired him to say those very words to his own father.

From the hospital Daniel called his aging dad and said the words his boy had said to him. "I forgive you, Dad."

Afterward Daniel was finally able to move forward, to find healing and help for his addictions, and to repair the broken relationship with his son.

God forgives us, and in turn he commands us to forgive one another.

TOOL TIP

Forgiving your loved ones benefits not only them but you as well. Forgiveness is at the foundation of any loving relationship.

THE COMMAND TO FORGIVE

We acknowledge that the Bible can be difficult to interpret and understand. But when it comes to the command to forgive, the Bible makes it very clear what is expected of Christians: "If you are standing before the altar in the Temple, offering a sacrifice to God, and you suddenly remember that someone has something against you, leave your sacrifice there beside the altar. Go and be reconciled to that person. Then come and offer your sacrifice to God" (Matthew 5:23-24, NLT).

It is next to impossible to have an open heart, a heart receptive to God's will, if we are in conflict with others. God desires a sincere gift from us, not one tarnished with unreconciled differences and past hurts. We are to make sure that people whom we have offended or who have offended us are freed from the bondage of anger, vengeance, or hate.

So, who are we to forgive? Is anyone excluded from receiving our forgiveness? Let's take a further look at Jesus' words in the fifth chapter of Matthew.

Loving Your Enemies

Jesus tells us that no one is above our forgiveness. He even makes a special point to command his followers to forgive their very worst enemies: "But I tell you: Love your enemies and pray for those who persecute you, that you may be sons of your Father in heaven. He causes his sun to rise on the evil and the good, and sends rain on the righteous and the unrighteous. If you love those who love you, what reward will you get? Are not even the tax collectors doing that? And if you greet only your brothers, what are you doing more than others? Do not even pagans do that? Be perfect, therefore, as your heavenly Father is perfect" (Matthew 5:44-48).

What a powerful passage about forgiveness!

These words touch on the very nature of our incredible God, who is merciful and gracious to all. We are called to be perfect, "as your heavenly Father is perfect." Even though we cannot be perfect while existing on this planet, we must strive for Christ's perfection. We must have Christ's willingness to love those who are unlovable; to care for people like the prostitutes, thieves, and tax collectors; to forgive people who offend us. Why should we forgive our enemies? God knows how unresolved anger kills the spirit within, and he designed this command to help free us from eternal regret.

The apostle Paul echoed Christ's command to love and forgive those we consider our enemies:

> If people persecute you because you are a Christian, don't curse them; pray that God will bless them. When others are happy, be happy with them. If they are sad, share their sorrow. Live in harmony with each other. Don't try to act important, but enjoy the company of ordinary people. And don't think you know it all! Never pay back evil for evil to anyone. Do things in such a way that everyone can see you are honorable. Do your part to live in peace with everyone, as much as possible. Dear friends, never avenge yourselves. Leave that to God. For it is written, "I will take vengeance; I will repay those who deserve it," says the

Lord. Instead, do what the Scriptures say: "If your enemies are hungry, feed them. If they are thirsty, give them something to drink, and they will be ashamed of what they have done to you." Don't let evil get the best of you, but conquer evil by doing good. (Romans 12:14-21)

And if God requires us to forgive our enemies, how much more important is it to him that we continually forgive those who are closest to us?

ROADBLOCKS TO FORGIVENESS

We all want to be happy in our relationships, and we know that means we must be willing to forgive. Still the question remains in many people's minds: "Why can't I forgive?"

We believe there are typically three main roadblocks to forgiveness.

1. The inability to see our own mistakes and imperfections. If we are unable to see our own faults and mistakes, how can we possibly move toward forgiveness in our relationships? We must first be able to admit that we are not perfect and that we are capable of hurting people we love.

2. Unresolved anger. Unresolved anger is a major hindrance to the healing power of forgiveness. If we refuse to let go of bitterness, rage, or hatred, we are holding on to very destructive forces. These forces are in direct contrast to the power of forgiveness, and they cannot exist together.

3. A misunderstanding about what forgiveness is. Finally, many people have great misconceptions about what forgiveness is, and therefore they struggle with it. Delusions about forgiveness are dangerous because they are not the truth. The truth will always set us free. But if we believe the lies about forgiveness, then we will refuse to forgive.

That brings us to what forgiveness is and what it is not. Let's start by clearing up one commonly held misconception about forgiveness.

WHAT IS FORGIVENESS?

One of the most common misconceptions about forgiveness is that it necessarily means forgetting. How many times have we heard someone say, "Forgive and forget!" This is next to impossible—barring serious brain injury, of course. We are not wired to completely forget painful events in our past.

Some people might think this kind of memory is God's cruel joke, just to torment us for our sins. On the contrary, it is a blessing that allows us to remember and learn from past experiences that were hurtful.

We don't believe it is possible to totally forget a hurt, but we also don't believe it's always a good thing to do so anyway. When we try to stuff away our hurts, we are only prolonging

WARNING:

Forgiving and forgetting are two different things.

the inevitable. When we do that, we are simply waiting for the explosion to occur. Like a volcano, the intense pressure from past hurts builds up inside us, looking for release until it finally erupts. And when it does, it is extremely damaging to family and friends.

The apostle James gives us a different approach to dealing with pain: "Consider it pure joy, my brothers, whenever you face trials of many kinds, because you know that the testing of your faith develops perseverance" (James 1:2-3).

James goes on to say that "perseverance must finish its work so that you may be mature and complete, not lacking anything" (v. 4). This means that trials and painful experiences—even within the relationships with those we love—are events that God can use in the maturation process of his people. Why would we want to forget?

William Meninger once wrote these words about forgiveness: "Forgiveness, then, is not forgetting. It is not condoning or absolving. Neither is it pretending nor something done for the sake of the offender. It is not a thing we just do by a brutal act of the will. It does not entail a loss of identity, of specialness, or of face. It does not release the offenders from obligations they may or may not recognize. An understanding of these things will go a long way towards helping people enter into the forgiveness process."[3]

FORGIVENESS: AN ONGOING PROCESS

Forgiveness is not a onetime event but a process. Unfortunately, many Christian men don't understand this. We Smalley guys often hear men tell us, "If she forgave me, then she would be over this by now!"

But come on, guys—that is not realistic. If you've done something extremely hurtful to your wife and are seeking her forgiveness, then you can't expect the healing to take place immediately. Your loved one may not get over the hurt right away. It may take time.

In fact—and this can be painful to consider—depending on the severity of the hurt, your loved one may never fully recover from the pain. This doesn't necessarily mean that you will suffer day after day for your wrongdoing or the wrongs done to you, but it does mean that the pain may show up from time to time, even years after the offense, usually when some event sparks the memory. The pain isn't as severe as when it first happened, but it still hurts.

We think this is one way God helps us to keep humble. It's hard to be overconfident about our emotional or spiritual maturity when we remember how things used to be. The great news is in James 1:2-4, where we are encouraged to remember that our pain only makes us better Christians.

GUY FACT

The average parent spends only nine minutes playing with his or her children on Christmas morning.

At one of our monthly marriage-enrichment seminars, a man approached us about a forgiveness issue. He was holding his wife's hand, and his eyes were reddened by the tears he'd shed. His wife looked ashamed, and we were about to find out why.

"I don't think I've forgiven my wife yet because I'm still hurt and angry over what she did to me," he said, grasping her hand in a tender and loving way to assure her that he loved her.

We were impressed by their obvious commitment to each other. Something in their eyes showed us they were in the marriage for the long haul. We asked the man what he needed to forgive his wife for, and in a matter of minutes he spilled out their story.

The man's wife had recently confessed to having multiple affairs during the first few years of their twenty-year marriage. She assured him that after those first few years, she'd never had another affair.

We were surprised that the wife could keep this secret from her husband for more than fifteen years. But then the hammer dropped, and we knew why she'd finally revealed her secret.

"It's possible that our fifteen-year-old daughter isn't mine," the man said.

We were amazed that he lovingly held his wife's hand, but what we learned next made that display of affection even more astonishing.

We asked the man exactly when he found out about the affairs and the possibility that his daughter may not actually be his. "Two weeks ago," he said calmly and with a straight face.

Two weeks! No wonder he hadn't fully forgiven his wife. How could he have expected to in so short a time?

The misunderstanding that forgiveness is immediate is a problem in the Christian community. We somehow believe that once we say those magic words, "I forgive you," all pain and hurt just disappear. But it doesn't always work that way. Often we must go through a process before we can completely heal from the hurt and forgive our loved one for the hurt he or she caused.

TOOL TIP

Forgiveness isn't a onetime event followed by bliss within a relationship. It is often a process.

What the Process of Forgiveness Looks Like

The process of forgiveness is just that, a process. But what does that process look like? We know we are commanded to forgive, but how do we do it?

We would like to discuss the forgiveness model of Christian psychiatrist Karl Menninger, who says that forgiveness is entirely in the hands of the victim. Although offenders can seek forgiveness, they do not control whether—or when—the offended person forgives.

If you choose to follow these next five steps to forgiveness, understand that you may move in and out of each level throughout the process. But along the way you will greatly increase your ability to forgive. Remember that forgiveness is a decision, a tool, and not a feeling, emotion, or accident.

STAGE ONE: CLAIMING THE HURT

The first step in the process of forgiveness, according to Menninger, is called "claiming the hurt." This means acknowledging that the offense was committed and that it caused you pain. After all, how can we forgive someone if we don't acknowledge that something needs to be forgiven?

This might seem obvious to many people. But keep in mind that living in denial or forgetfulness is much easier for some people than admitting something painful has happened. In psychology it's called the "pleasure principle," and it means that we humans behave in a way that maximizes pleasure and minimizes pain. In other words, we don't want to suffer pain, so we avoid it by ignoring it, disguising it, hiding it, stuffing it, or using a whole host of defense mechanisms.

The first step to forgiveness is seeing what pain does in our lives. It's about opening our eyes and not living in denial. This is important because it means we've admitted that someone has done something to us and needs to be forgiven in order for the relationship to be restored.

STAGE TWO: HANDLING MISPLACED GUILT

Now that you've claimed the hurt, it's time to deal with your guilt. It is actually common for the one who has been wronged to feel somewhat responsible for what happened. That person may ask himself or herself, "What could I have done to prevent my hurt?" or "If only I hadn't . . ." Both thoughts are very normal and necessary in the process of forgiveness.

By recognizing your hurts, you give yourself the opportunity to have power over them by proactively doing something about them. You now know what is causing your emotional pain. It helps during this stage of the process to do something that makes you feel valuable.

Victims of hurt often feel worthless and powerless, and doing something specifically for yourself will help bring you out of the guilt stage. Get active during this process. You have to *do* something, move in a direction in order for change to occur.

Couples in therapy sometimes wonder why things aren't getting better for them. But then they realize they are doing the same things that got them into trouble in the first place. In order to enjoy real and lasting change, we have to change our behavior. Menninger encourages us to ask God to remind us of our value in him and why being created in his image is such an awesome gift.

STAGE THREE: FEELING VICTIMIZED

You've claimed the hurt and experienced the misplaced possible guilt. The next stage is when you feel like a victim. Once you recognize your hurt, it's only natural to feel victimized. Signs of this stage are depression, listlessness, isolation, or bitterness.

When we suffer these kinds of emotions, many of us tend to "medicate" them using drugs, alcohol, food—anything that makes us feel momentarily better. But these "fixes" are only momentary.

This stage is a cry for help—it's a 911 to your soul. The best thing to do at this stage is join a support group and do things for other people. Helping others helps yourself.

STAGE FOUR: ANGER

Many people may want to ignore their feelings of anger because they've been taught that anger is a bad thing. But anger is not bad or wrong or evil. In fact, anger can be extremely healthy if it is handled in a healthy way.

Anger motivates us to change and take action. It can be like the fuel in the process of forgiveness. It gives us the energy we need to make it through the process of forgiveness.

But what is inappropriate anger?

When anger is focused on vengeance, then it is not a healthy anger. Anger shouldn't be motivated by a need to get back at somebody. Healthy anger is motivated by a need to change something about the relationship. Vengeance will destroy us. It's like toxic waste to the soul. Its very nature is hateful, which is not in God's plan.

Paul wrote in Ephesians 4:26, "Be angry, and do not sin" (NKJV). We sin in our anger when we hold on to it. And when we don't want to let our anger go, it takes root in our souls and blocks our relationship with God and our loved ones. Positive anger lets us know something needs to be taken care of. It's like the warning lights in your car. When they're blinking, you'd better take notice of the problem. The writer of the book of Hebrews put it this way: "See to it that no one misses the grace of God and that no bitter root grows up to cause trouble and defile many" (12:15). Pent-up anger might not cause problems right away, but let us assure you, it will grow, and someday it will hurt the people around you.

STAGE FIVE: WHOLENESS AND FORGIVENESS

When you reach the fifth stage of forgiveness, you are actually ready to forgive fully because you have had the opportunity to grow through the previous four stages. You're no longer a victim of your pain because you've taken control over it.

Forgiveness is the ultimate sign of maturity and love. Forgiveness says that I know you're not perfect but neither am I, so I choose to love you and forgive you. Now I am free to grow in the magnificence of God.

Wholeness is a direct product of the first four stages. It's not even a choice, but a product of the first four stages of forgiveness. You don't grab on to wholeness; it grabs you. And in the process you can repair just about any relationship.

We want to cover one more point about forgiveness: our need to ask our loved one's forgiveness when we've wronged her.

SEEKING FORGIVENESS

The need to seek forgiveness is a normal part of a love relationship. You will experience times of hardship or emotional strain in any relationship, but as long as you are committed to seeking forgiveness from one an-other when it's needed, the hard times can become benefits, not deficits.

In other words, at some time or another you will need to seek for-giveness from your loved one. And when doing that, keep three things in mind.

1. Take care with your approach. Remember that the way you ap-proach your loved one sets the tone of the conversation. Your voice should be soft, and you should be receptive to the other person's feel-ings and attitude. Everything needs to be soft—from tender touch to the sincerity communicated in your voice.

When you prepare to approach someone and seek his or her for-giveness, you need to go with humility and without an attitude of de-fensiveness. The three of us like to ask ourselves, "How humble am I right now?" or "How willing am I to hear what others might say?" If we have rehearsed our rebuttal, we're probably not ready.

Most of all, you need to avoid placing blame on the other person. Too often we want to blame others for the hurt *we* cause. But doing that only invalidates our loved ones, and invalidation is a major factor in the failure of relationships.

2. Be clear on the damage done. Start by asking specifically how you have hurt your loved one. Often our idea of what we've done to hurt our loved one is wrong. Taking the time to find out specifically how you have caused the hurt is a major step toward validating your loved one's feelings and needs.

This allows the person we love to communicate her feelings, and if she doesn't want to do that at the moment, then take time to let her or-ganize her thoughts. You can even ask questions to help her understand more clearly how you have hurt her.

3. Worry only about your own faults. When you know you have hurt your loved one, don't waste your energy worrying about what he or she has done to you. You can't control other people, and you can't make them seek forgiveness or accept your forgiveness.

By humbly seeking forgiveness and acknowledging every aspect of wrongdoing on your part, you are taking care of your own responsibilities. God does not hold us responsible for our spouse's sin, only our own.

Well, that about ends our shopping trip. We've explored the benefits of our internal tools—the ones that make us natural providers and protectors—and we've recognized the fact that we may need to add some tools to our relational toolboxes. We've walked through the Bible, the Home Depot of relational tools, and picked up six basic relational tools that will help us build solid, happy relationships. We've even taken a close look at how to use those relational tools. And finally, we've explored the importance of using forgiveness to repair broken bonds with those we love.

Now it's time to leave the store and get to work.

Happy building!

Study Guide

Discuss the following questions with other guys in a discussion group, or use them just for your own growth. See them as accessories to help you take some steps toward putting the relational tools to use.

1. Which of the internal tools do you most relate to? Why?
   Fact-giving tool
   Fact-finding tool
   Take-charge tool
   Task-oriented tool
   Problem-solving tool
   Competitive-drive tool
2. Give examples of times when these tools have helped you.
3. What are you good at?
4. Which of the internal tools help make you good at that?
5. Which of these internal tools make you independent, putting stress on your relationships?
6. How does that independence influence your significant relationships?
7. Think about your relationships. List three relationships that need to be built up or repaired:

   _____

   _____

   _____

8. Why haven't those relationships been successful in the past?
9. Which internal tools have you been using in these relationships? Give an example.
10. In your own words, describe the relational toolbox. Why is it important that men have relational tools?

11. Why don't these relational tools come naturally to men?
12. Which relational tools deal with communicating?
13. Give an example of how you can use the open-sharing tool to build better foundations in your relationships.
14. Give an example of how you can use the patient-listening tool to build better foundations in your relationships.
15. Which relational tools deal with behavior?
16. Give an example of how you can use the win-win tool to build better relationships.
17. Give an example of how you can use the selfless-honor tool to build better relationships.
18. Give an example of how you can use the tender-touch tool to build better relationships.
19. Give an example of how you can use the time-and-energy tool to build better relationships.
20. Which loved ones do you need to forgive? Which ones do you need to seek forgiveness from? Explain how you might do this using the relational tools.

Notes

Chapter 2: A Man's Internal Tools
1. "UCLA Researchers Identify Key Biobehavioral Pattern Used by Women to Manage Stress"; <www.college.ucla.edu/stress.htm>.
2. Rae André, *Positive Solitude* (New York: HarperCollins, 1991).

Chapter 3: Looking Back: Where Did These Tools Come From?
1. Minnesota Family Council, "Polls Show Women Want More Time with Their Children" (November 2001); <www.mfc.org/contents/article.asp?id=299>.
2. Ibid.
3. Pew Research Center for the People and the Press, *Motherhood Today—A Tougher Job, Less Ably Done* (May 9, 1997): 1.
4. David C. Geary, "Sex Differences in Brain and Cognition," *Male, Female: The Evolution of Human Sex Differences* (Washington, D.C.: American Psychological Association, 1998).

Chapter 4: Testosterone: Why Guys Are Good at Being Guys
1. Anne Moir and David Jessel, *Brain Sex: The Real Difference between Men and Women* (New York: Dell, 1989), 21–38.
2. Ibid.
3. Ibid., 50–52.
4. Eugene Shippen and William Fryer, *The Testosterone Syndrome: The Critical Factor for Energy, Health, and Sexuality* (New York: M. Evans, 1998), 15.

Chapter 6: Why Guys Have Trouble with Conversations
1. Nancy M. Henley and Cheris Kramarae, "Gender, Power, and Miscommunication," *Variations in the Form and Use of Language,* ed. Ralph W. Fasold (Washington, D.C.: Georgetown University Press, 1983), 3.

Chapter 7: Why Guys Have Trouble Bonding
1. Michael G. Conner, "Understanding the Difference between Men and Women"; <www.crisiscounseling.com/Relationships/DifferencesMenWomen.htm>.

Chapter 8: Reaching for the Right Tools
1. Dean Ornish, *Love and Survival* (New York: HarperCollins, 1998), 61.
2. Ibid., 14.

Chapter 9: Adding to Your Relational Toolbox: One-Stop Shopping
1. Dean Ornish, *Love and Survival* (New York: HarperCollins, 1998), 58–59.

Chapter 10: Building the Foundation through Communication
1. For more help with word pictures, read Gary Smalley and John Trent, *The Language of Love* (Waco, Tex.: Word, 1988).
2. Deborah Tannen, *You Just Don't Understand* (New York: Morrow, 1990).

Chapter 12: Forgiveness: The Tool for Repairing Any Relationship
1. I first told this story in my book *Joy That Lasts* (Grand Rapids: Zondervan, 1988) as an illustration of my quest to find satisfaction in the wrong places, in position and possessions rather than in God.
2. Through that relational crisis I learned some powerful life lessons and eventually came to a place of personal freedom as well as freedom in the relationship. While Dale's treatment of me needed adjustment, my heart needed even more. You can read about the profound changes I experienced in *Joy That Lasts*.
3. William Meninger, *The Process of Forgiveness* (New York: Continuum, 1996), 33.

About the Authors

DR. GARY SMALLEY, founder and chairman of the board of the Smalley Relationship Center, is one of the country's best-known authors and speakers on family relationships. He is the author and coauthor of more than forty books, including the best-selling, award-winning books *Marriage for a Lifetime, Secrets to Lasting Love, The Blessing* (with John Trent), *The Two Sides of Love* (with John Trent), and *The Language of Love* (with John Trent). Recent releases include *Bound by Honor* (with his son Greg Smalley), *Food and Love, One Flame, Food and Love Cookbook,* and the Redemption fiction series (with Karen Kingsbury). Gary has also produced several popular films and videos.

Gary has appeared on national television programs such as *The Oprah Winfrey Show, Larry King Live,* the *Today* show, *Sally Jessy Raphael,* as well as numerous national radio programs. Gary has been featured on hundreds of regional and local television and radio programs across the United States.

In addition to earning a master's degree from Bethel Theological Seminary, Gary has received two honorary doctorates, one from Biola University (California) and one from Southwest Baptist University (Missouri), for his work with couples.

Gary and his wife, Norma, have been married for nearly forty years and live in Branson, Missouri. They have been blessed with eight grandchildren.

DR. GREG SMALLEY earned his doctorate in clinical psychology from Rosemead School of Psychology at Biola University in southern California. He also holds a master's degree in counseling psychology from Denver Seminary. Dr. Smalley is the president and CEO of the Smalley

Relationship Center, located in Branson, Missouri. He teaches at the monthly Marriage for a Lifetime marriage seminars across the country. He has appeared on television and radio programs, including *Focus on the Family* and *Hour of Power*. He has published more than one hundred articles about parenting and relationship issues for *Living with Teenagers, Shine, Homes of Honor, Christian Parenting Today, ParentLife, HonorBound,* and *Branson Living.* Greg is the coauthor of *Bound by Honor* (with Gary Smalley) as well as *Winning Your Wife Back* and *Winning Your Husband Back* (both with Gary Smalley and Deborah Smalley). Greg and his wife, Erin, are the parents of two daughters, Taylor and Maddy, and a son, Garrison. The family lives in Branson, Missouri.

MICHAEL SMALLEY, who holds a master's degree in clinical psychology from Wheaton College Graduate School, is a speaker for the Smalley Relationship Center and maintains a counseling practice working with individuals, couples, and families in Branson, Missouri. During the past eight years he has spoken live to more than one million people and has appeared on numerous radio and television shows such as *At Home—Live!* (with Chuck and Jenni Borsellino), *LIFE TODAY* (with James Robison), and the *Warren Duffy Show*. His message is simple and applicable to anyone in any situation: Honor God and others above yourself. Michael and his wife, Amy, have three children and work with the youth group at Woodland Hills Community Church.

SMALLEY RELATIONSHIP CENTER

Our mission is to create a marriage revival throughout the world by increasing marital satisfaction and reducing the divorce rate.

ENRICHMENT PRODUCTS

The Smalley Relationship Center has more than 50 marriage, parenting, and relational books, videos, and audiotapes to enrich all of your most important relationships.

SMALLEY ON-LINE

Our Web site provides weekly e-newsletters, new articles on marriage and parenting, interviews with authors, and on-line enrichment through marriage and personality profiles. Preview or order our latest resources.

ENRICHMENT EVENTS

We offer events with nationally known speakers as well as our own speaking team. Events include nationwide Couples Conferences through satellite technology, special live conferences that focus on specific needs, workshops for continuing education, and much more!

COUNSELING SERVICES

INTENSIVE MARRIAGE COUNSELING — During the "intensive" you and your spouse will spend two days (Marriage Intensive) or four days (Couples Intensive) with our marriage specialists in Branson, Missouri. This concentrated time allows you to rapidly move down to the root of your problems in a way that traditional weekly therapy  cannot duplicate. The Intensive programs have had remarkable success with couples in crisis.

PROJECT SMALL GROUP

We are calling men and women to become "Marriage Champions" by taking the step of becoming marriage small group leaders. Our Web site offers not only eight different series that you or your church can order but also support for leaders.

PHONE COUNSELING — Are you having trouble finding a Christian counselor in your area? Do you want to work with a pastoral counselor who knows how to apply the teachings of the Smalleys? Phone counseling might be the perfect fit. Our trained professional counselors are standing by.

To contact us, call 800-848-6329 or visit www.smalleyonline.com